10 RULES FOR RAISING KIDS IN A HIGH-TECH WORLD

ALSO BY JEAN TWENGE

Generations

iGen

Generation Me

The Impatient Woman's Guide to Getting Pregnant

The Narcissism Epidemic (coauthor)

10 RULES FOR RAISING KIDS IN A HIGH-TECH WORLD

How Parents Can Stop Smartphones, Social Media, and Gaming from Taking Over Their Children's Lives

DR JEAN M TWENGE

Vermilion
LONDON

VERMILION

UK | USA | Canada | Ireland | Australia
India | New Zealand | South Africa

Vermilion is part of the Penguin Random House group of companies whose addresses can be found at global.penguinrandomhouse.com

Penguin Random House UK
One Embassy Gardens, 8 Viaduct Gardens, London SW11 7BW

penguin.co.uk
global.penguinrandomhouse.com

Penguin Random House UK

First published by Atria Books in 2025
This edition published by Vermilion in 2025
1

Interior design by Kris Tobiassen

Typeset by Six Red Marbles UK, Thetford, Norfolk

Printed and bound in Great Britain by Clays Ltd, Elcograf S.p.A.

The authorised representative in the EEA is Penguin Random House Ireland, Morrison Chambers, 32 Nassau Street, Dublin D02 YH68

A CIP catalogue record for this book is available from the British Library

ISBN 9781785046407

MIX
Paper | Supporting responsible forestry
FSC www.fsc.org FSC® C018179

Penguin Random House is committed to a sustainable future for our business, our readers and our planet. This book is made from Forest Stewardship Council® certified paper.

For Kate, Navy Corpsman and Class of '29,
who made me the parent of an adult

CONTENTS

Introduction: The need for rules • 1

Rule 1: You're in charge • 19

Rule 2: No electronic devices in the bedroom overnight • 35

Rule 3: No social media until age 16—or later • 49

Rule 4: First phones should be basic phones • 73

Rule 5: Give the first smartphone with the driver's license • 89

Rule 6: Use parental controls • 97

Rule 7: Create no-phone zones • 113

Rule 8: Give your kids real-world freedom • 125

Rule 9: Beware the laptop—and the gaming console, and the tablet, and . . . • 149

Rule 10: Advocate for no phones during the school day • 167

Conclusion: You've got this • 183

Acknowledgments • 185

Notes • 189

Index • 205

INTRODUCTION: THE NEED FOR RULES

When Dany Elachi's daughter, Aalia, was 10, she told him she was the only one in her class without a smartphone, and that if she didn't get one she'd be left out. "After a few weeks of persistent pleading, we handed young Aalia her first smartphone," Dany says. "She suddenly wasn't playing with her younger siblings as much. Novels were promptly cast aside. She wasn't around to help with dinner anymore. She danced less, laughed less. She was quieter, our home was quieter. Within a matter of weeks, the screen wedded to her palm had literally transformed her childhood."

Parents are not the only ones noticing how smartphones and social media have changed childhood. Teens know it, too. Kate Romalewski also got her first smartphone at age 10. "I spent hours finding the perfect photos to post on Instagram, analyzing selfies of my prepubescent face for imperfections," she recalled at 17. "I was a ball of anxiety. I remember looking in the mirror and wishing I was somebody else. I hated social media and recognized how awful it made me feel, but I could not put it down." Sixteen-year-old Luke Martin said,

"Social media is built around FOMO [fear of missing out], so I felt like I couldn't get off it . . . it was a downward spiral." He eventually decided to swap his smartphone for a "dumbphone" with only calling, texting, and maps.

For the past two decades, I've traveled the country giving talks on generational differences to college faculty, military leaders, and corporate managers. After my book *iGen* was published in 2017, I started giving talks to parent groups as well. Before long, though, the questions from these different audiences started to blur together. No matter what the group, a version of one question always came up in the first few minutes of the Q&A: *What should I do about my kids and their technology use?*

I'm the parent of three. I know where that question comes from: love—and desperation.

Parents are drowning. So are kids. Younger and younger kids are using social media. Virtually every teen has a smartphone, and many can't put it down. Some kids would play video games every waking hour if they could.

It often feels like the whole world is conspiring to keep our kids tethered to tech—and that's because it is. Social media companies have poured billions of dollars into making their products as addictive as possible, especially for kids and teens. Smartphones are convenient and ubiquitous, and answering a friend's text right away seems mandatory. School laptops are great for doing homework, but also great for watching videos and telling Mom or Dad you're doing homework when you're not.

These new technologies are barely regulated. Children 12 and under are not supposed to have social media accounts, but they can simply lie about their birth year to sign up. When states have passed laws requiring age verification, tech companies have immediately sued to keep the laws from going into effect. Kids and teens can just click on a button labeled "I am 18 or older—Enter" to access pornography websites. For the foreseeable future, keeping kids safe online is up to parents.

That's a daunting job, but not an impossible one. Every parent instinctively knows there's something more they could be or should be doing—that's why they are asking these questions at my events, and seeking answers online and in books. Unfortunately, much of what's out there is vague. It says rules are going to differ based on the kid or the family. It says you should teach your kids "digital literacy," whatever that means. It says limits should depend on what kids are doing online, even though that can change by the minute. It says we should talk to kids about why they shouldn't spend too much time on their phones—and then expect them to put down their phone at bedtime and stop spending so much time on social media.

As any parent of teens will tell you, this doesn't work. We need something that does.

That's where this book comes in, with 10 concrete rules about how to manage kids and the technology that surrounds them—and all of us. These are not anti-tech rules. They are rules that make sure kids are ready before we give them phones, social media, and free rein online. They're rules that ensure technology doesn't take over our children's lives. The rules are:

Rule 1: You're in charge

Rule 2: No electronic devices in the bedroom overnight

Rule 3: No social media until age 16—or later

Rule 4: First phones should be basic phones

Rule 5: Give the first smartphone with the driver's license

Rule 6: Use parental controls

Rule 7: Create no-phone zones

Rule 8: Give your kids real-world freedom

Rule 9: Beware the laptop—and the gaming console, and the tablet, and . . .

Rule 10: Advocate for no phones during the school day

When my kids were young, someone said to me, "Remember: You're not raising children. You're raising adults." I have thought about that nearly every day since. Parenting means thinking long-term about what our kids need for their mental health, growth, and development, not just what they want short-term to amuse themselves or fit in with their friends. It's about setting kids up for success today *and* tomorrow. It's about creating a firewall for kids against anxiety, attention issues, and constant insecurity. It's about crafting habits and values in families that wire kids' brains for resilience, success, and contentment. In today's tech-saturated world, having rules around devices is one of the best ways to do that.

THE REASONS

Why is it so important to set rules around devices? Some parents have seen the effects of devices on their children firsthand and don't need to see the research before putting rules in place. Others want to know what the research says. I'll share a brief overview of what we know about the effects of growing up in our technology-infused age. The Notes section at the end of the book includes the sources if you'd like to learn more.

I first became interested in kids and tech when my own children were very young, years before they or their peers had smartphones or social media. It all started with some strange research results.

At that point, in the early 2010s, I had already spent more than two decades researching generational differences, analyzing large surveys of American teens done every year since the 1970s. I got used to seeing trends that would build gradually over a decade or two.

Then sudden spikes started to appear, especially in mental health and happiness. Beginning around 2012, more teens started to say they felt lonely and left out. More started to say they felt like they couldn't do anything right, or that their lives didn't feel useful—classic symptoms of depression. Teens' happiness and satisfaction with life declined. This happened eight years *before* COVID (for example, see Figure 0.1 on the following page).

At first, I had no idea what might be causing these abrupt changes. The economy was on an upswing, and it was difficult to think of an event around 2012 that kept building from there. But then I realized it: Teen depression spiked right as smartphones and social media were becoming popular. Smartphone ownership in the U.S. first reached 50% at the end of 2012; 2012 was also the year Facebook bought Instagram. In 2009, less than half of teens used social media every day,

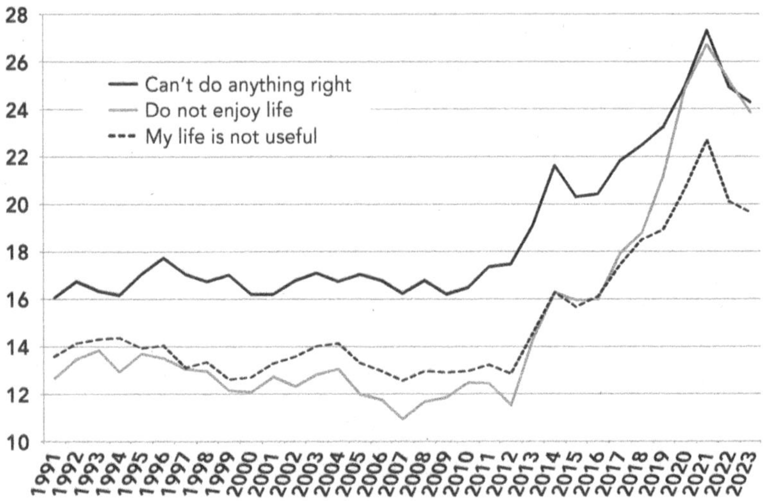

Figure 0.1: Symptoms of depression, U.S. teens, 1991–2023

Source: Monitoring the Future survey of 8th, 10th, and 12th graders
Note: The 2020 data were collected in February and early March before pandemic lockdowns.

mostly on a computer. By 2017, 85% did, usually on their own phones, anytime, anywhere.

Plus, time on devices was replacing in-person socializing—teens weren't going to the movies, hanging out with friends, or going to parties as much as previous generations (for example, see Figure 0.2 on the following page). Teens' social lives went from mostly in-person to mostly online.

Teens also weren't sleeping as much. The number who were sleeping more than seven hours a night declined sharply right around 2012 (see Figure 0.3 on the following page). Teens need about nine hours of sleep a night, so seven hours is a pretty low bar. Less than half of 12th graders were regularly getting this much sleep after 2014, and by 2020 less than half of 10th graders were. Devices were interfering with kids' sleep, and sleep deprivation is a well-established cause of depression and unhappiness.

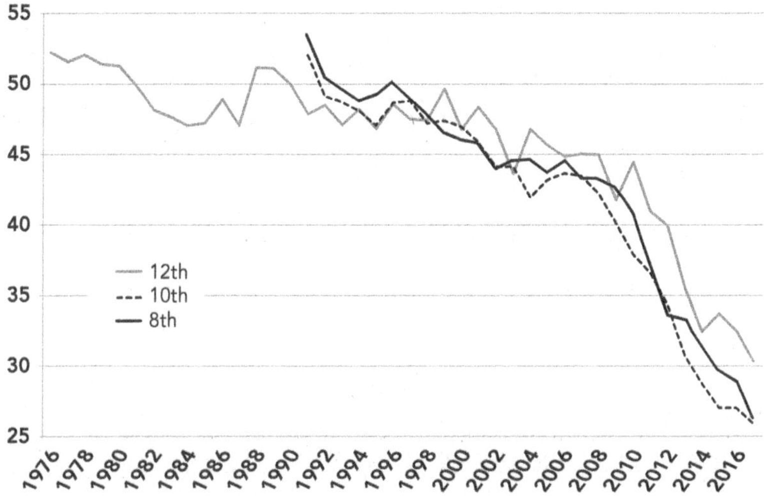

Figure 0.2: Percent of U.S. teens who get together with their friends almost every day, 1976–2017

Source: Monitoring the Future survey of 8th, 10th, and 12th graders

Note: The wording of this item changed after 2018, so only data up to 2017 is shown here.

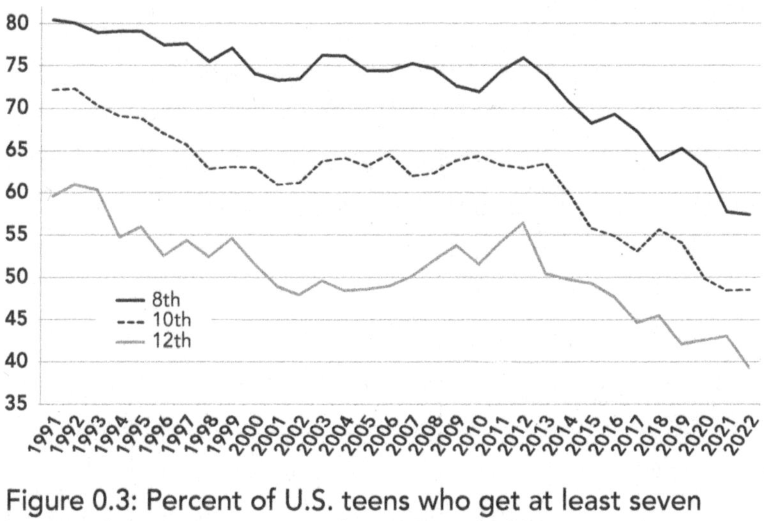

Figure 0.3: Percent of U.S. teens who get at least seven hours of sleep on most nights, 1976–2023

Source: Monitoring the Future survey of 8th, 10th, and 12th graders

In my 2017 book, *iGen: Why Today's Super-Connected Kids Are Growing Up Less Rebellious, More Tolerant, Less Happy—and Completely Unprepared for Adulthood*, I theorized that depression rose because teens were spending more time online, less time with friends in person, and less time sleeping—a terrible formula for mental health. An excerpt of *iGen* in *The Atlantic*, headlined "Have Smartphones Destroyed a Generation?," went viral.

Since then, the popularity and impact of these new technologies has only grown. Half of teens said they were online "almost constantly" by 2022. By 2023, according to Gallup, the average American teen spent almost five hours a day using social media. Rates of clinical-level depression among teens doubled by 2019. Depression increased further during the COVID-19 pandemic, but those upticks paled in comparison to the surge that started in the early 2010s (see Figure 0.4 on the following page).

The number of teens with mental health issues also increased internationally. Around the world, more teens said they felt lonely at school starting around 2012—the same pattern as in the U.S. In Europe and English-speaking countries, rates of anxiety and depression also spiked among teens after 2012.

The trends weren't limited to symptoms; they also appeared in worrisome behaviors linked to mental health issues. The number of 10- to 14-year-old girls admitted to the emergency room for self-harm in the U.S. quintupled between 2009 and 2022. Most tragic of all, twice as many 10- to 14-year-olds took their own lives via suicide. Every time I see these statistics, I think about the parents who are desperately trying to stop their 11-year-old daughter from harming herself again

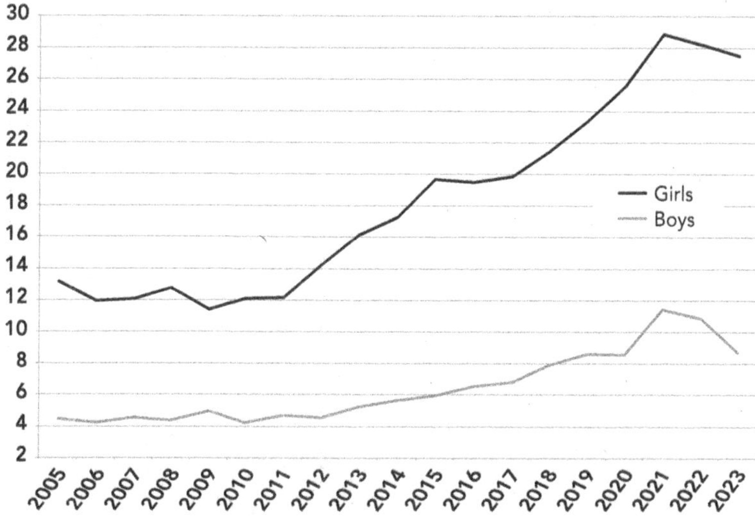

Figure 0.4: Rates of clinical-level depression, U.S. 12- to 17-year-olds, 2005–2023

Source: National Survey on Drug Use and Health

Note: Depression rates are the percentage suffering from a major depressive episode in the last year. This is a screening study taking a cross-section of the whole population, not just those who seek treatment. Thus the increases cannot be due to more willingness to seek help or to overdiagnosis.

and the devastated families missing beloved children. The numbers are staggering, and they aren't just numbers.

These trends show what's happened in the generation as a whole. But is there a link between more device use and more depression among individual teens? There is. In one of the best-designed studies, girls who were heavy users of social media were three times as likely to be depressed as nonusers (see Figure 0.5 on the following page). Boys who were heavy users were twice as likely to be depressed.

Across dozens of studies, teens who are heavy users of screen media (electronic games, the internet, online videos, and social media) are between 30% and 200% more likely to

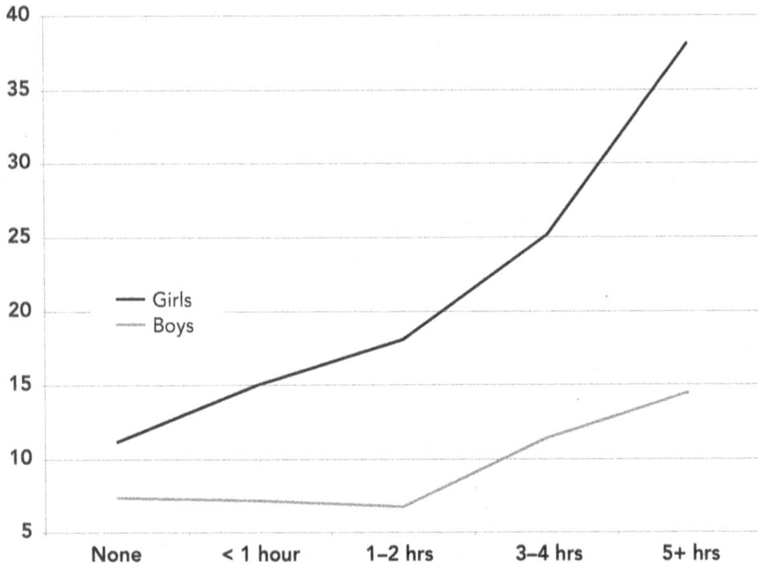

Figure 0.5: Social media use and depression, UK teens

Source: Kelly et al. (2019), Millennium Cohort Study

be depressed or unhappy than their peers who are on screens less often. Sometimes the link is larger for social media and internet time than for gaming and videos, but the association is nearly always there.

When people cut back on social media for a few weeks, they end up happier and less depressed compared to those who keep using social media as they always have. A study of Danish families found that after two weeks with minimal access to screens, kids and teens were less angry and less depressed compared to a control group who did not change their screen use. These studies are experiments (also known as randomized controlled trials), the gold standard in science for showing causation because people are randomly assigned to either cut back on social media time or not, which equalizes extraneous factors. These studies mean social media causes depression, not just that the two are linked. In June 2024, the U.S. Surgeon General called for warning labels to be placed on social media to make parents aware of their potential harm to teens' mental health.

The stories behind the statistics are harrowing. When Alexis Spence was 11, she opened an Instagram account on her iPad without her parents knowing. As Alexis consumed more and more "thinspiration" content, she began starving herself. By 15, she had developed a severe eating disorder and spent time in a residential treatment center as she battled anorexia and suicidal thoughts. Alexis survived, but still struggles with mental health issues and was not able to leave home for college.

A blackmailer posing as a teen girl talked a 15-year-old Utah boy into sending nude pictures of himself on Snapchat. The user threatened to send screenshots of the images to his friends and family unless he paid $200. He was so devastated he took his own life.

Selena Rodriquez opened an Instagram account when she was 10 and before long was using it at all hours of the day and night. When she wasn't on Instagram, she was on Snapchat. Several adult men asked her to send nude pictures and videos of herself. Selena was eventually hospitalized for depression and self-harm. At the age of 11, she died by suicide.

These stories involve severe outcomes that won't happen to most kids. But these tragedies are the tip of the iceberg, with many more kids experiencing less extreme but still concerning outcomes after using social media heavily, including lack of sleep, depression, body image issues, cyberbullying, and obsessive use. Nevertheless, social media use by children and teens is virtually unregulated. Age isn't verified, and parental permission is not required. Social media companies say they try to take down negative content, but cyberbullying, pornography, sexual exploitation, references to drugs, and other dangers persist. According to Snapchat's own research, one in four 13- to 15-year-olds have been asked to share explicit pictures of themselves, and about the same number have received such images.

WHY RULES?

Until social media is regulated more, it's up to parents to protect their kids. As former Surgeon General Dr. Vivek Murthy put it, "There is no seatbelt for parents to click, no helmet to snap in place, no assurance that trusted experts have investigated and ensured that these platforms are safe for our kids. There are just parents and their children, trying to figure it out on their own, pitted against some of the best product engineers and most well-resourced companies in the world." Until laws change or social norms shift, parents are the first and sometimes the only line of defense against devices taking over their children's lives.

The impacts of tech go far beyond mental health. With kids and teens spending less time with their friends in person, their social skills are suffering. Kids are inside on their devices instead of outside in the real world, robbing them of experiences with independence and decision-making. Parents and children spend less time together, interfering with family bonding. Teens are distracted at school by their phones, can't concentrate on their homework, and arrive at college unable to focus long enough to read a few pages in a textbook. Children are exposed to sexual content and are contacted by unknown adults online long before they are ready.

With so little regulation and so much peer pressure for kids to not be "the only one" who doesn't have a smartphone or social media, parents are struggling. These issues are cropping up earlier and earlier, with elementary school kids now using TikTok and sporting their own smartphones. It seems like technology is everywhere, always sinking its claws into our kids.

But that doesn't mean we should give up. It *is* possible to protect kids from the worst aspects of today's intrusive and immersive technology. You just need a few rules—not halfway or squishy rules, not "let's talk to kids about good digital citizenship" rules, not "it depends" rules, but concrete rules for how to stem the digital tide and keep our kids healthy and happy. Best of all, these are not Luddite "no-tech-ever" mandates. Instead, these suggestions are designed to help your kids participate in the modern tech world but not be overwhelmed by it at a young age.

The rules are all based on research, and the implementation is based on my experiences with my own kids and what I've learned from talking to thousands of parents, teachers, and kids during visits to schools over the last eight years. I'll share both the successes (to pass on what works) and the mistakes (so you won't make the same ones). In each chapter, I'll give the reasons behind the rule and specific advice on how to follow it. There's also a section on common obstacles and pushbacks, so you know how to work around issues as they crop up and counter arguments your kids or others might make.

What if you can follow only some of the rules? That's OK. Even if you can just get your kids' devices out of their bedrooms overnight (Rule 2), you'll have a positive impact. There are good reasons behind each of the rules, but time and resources are limited and sometimes partway is as far as you're going to get. Partway is much better than nothing.

What if you make mistakes? I certainly did. But I tried to correct them. There's a saying that applies here: "Don't let the perfect be the enemy of the good." In other words, don't give up on the good the rules can do even if you can't follow them perfectly all the time. Nobody is perfect, and that's especially true in parenting. And that, too, is OK.

Before we get in deeper, a note on terms. I'll use the term *kids* to refer to both children and teens as it's more concise. Just realize that when I say "kids" that includes teens. When I'm using examples from my own family, I'll refer to my children by their first initials—from oldest to youngest, they are K, E, and J. When I began writing this book, they were ages 17, 14, and 12. I'll use the term *device* to mean an electronic device; that's usually a smartphone, laptop, tablet, or gaming console. A *smartphone* means a phone with internet access. That's in contrast to a *basic phone*, a phone without internet or social media (not all of these are old-school flip phones, as you'll see in Rule 4).

THE LIMITS OF TALKING

So why do we need rules in the first place? Why not just *talk* to our kids about how they use devices?

Of course we should talk to our kids, and I encourage you to share the insights in this book with them. When I relate research and stories about the downsides of devices, it's not just to convince you—it's also to help you convince your kids. Likewise, it's great to discuss the upsides of devices, like what your kids like doing online and what they get out of it. You can then talk to them about healthy limits and potential dangers.

That said, education is not enough. It's not enough to simply talk to kids about keeping their phones outside their bedrooms at night. It's not enough to tell kids they might see inappropriate or harmful content online. It's not enough to advise that they shouldn't be spending three hours a day on TikTok.

They need rules.

They need rules because they are kids. As a society, we have many rules in place to protect kids and teens as they grow up. The prefrontal cortex, which is in charge of self-control and decision-making, develops more slowly than the rest of the brain and isn't fully formed until the mid-20s. This is why teens do dumb things sometimes. That's why we age-gate activities that are dangerous, addictive, or require solid judgment. It's why in most of the world 13-year-olds are not allowed to drive, 15-year-olds are not allowed to vote, and 16-year-olds are not allowed to buy alcohol.

Imagine if we said, "Let's just *talk* to kids about why they shouldn't drink alcohol until they are older. But we're not going to check their IDs if they want to buy it. And why not just leave the whiskey bottles out when they're having friends over for a party? We talked to them about why they shouldn't drink until they're older. And they learned about 'alcohol literacy' at school!" This would never fly, because kids aren't ready to decide for themselves whether to drink alcohol. That's why most countries don't allow kids under 18 (and under 21 in the U.S.) to buy alcohol, and why IDs are checked. Will some kids still get their hands on alcohol? Unfortunately yes, but we also don't have 11-year-olds walking out of liquor stores with three bottles of Wild Turkey. Why? Because we've done more than just talk to kids about it. We have rules.

The government imposing age-gating for buying alcohol helps parents enforce rules around underage drinking. That's unfortunately not true for devices and social media, but the same principle applies: Parents must set boundaries to protect kids and teens from themselves. Author Scott Galloway, who has two teen sons, puts it this way: "My job as their dad is to be their prefrontal cortex until it shows up."

Kids also need rules because social media apps and gaming companies have spent billions of dollars to make their products as addictive as possible. This is why even middle-aged adults spend way too much time on Facebook. Sean Parker, one of Facebook's founders, said, "It's a social validation feedback loop . . . you're exploiting a vulnerability in human psychology. We understood this, consciously, and we did it anyway." When Facebook was being developed, he says, the objective was "How do we consume as much of your time and conscious attention as possible?" And that was before social media companies started using algorithms to feed people the content that would keep them tethered to the app.

Kids are especially susceptible to these techniques as they have yet to develop mature self-control. In adolescence, friendship and status are all-important, making it even harder to stay away from the apps. Social media companies have invested in algorithms for a very simple reason: The more time users spend on the app, the more money they make. And if they can get them young, the company will make more money over the user's lifetime. That might be why nearly half of teens say they are online "almost constantly." The companies know this: TikTok's internal research, for example, concluded that minors have "minimal ability to self-regulate effectively" and "do not have executive function to control their screen time."

Let me get this out of the way: It is completely unfair, not to mention difficult and stressful, that parents are expected to shoulder the entire burden of protecting kids online. It is unconscionable that kids can open social media accounts as soon as they can read, that they can access pornography by simply clicking a button saying they are 18, and that unknown adults can easily contact kids on social media sites. The sites themselves are not going to take serious steps to protect kids, as that will harm their profits. Until regulations change—and it doesn't look like that's happening anytime soon—it's up to parents. Yes, that's unfair, but it's also the reality.

This reality is why we need rules. Here are 10.

RULE 1: YOU'RE IN CHARGE

Imagine that when you were a kid you went to your parents and said, "Now that I'm 10, I want you to buy me a gadget that costs $1,000 plus $40 for every month I have it. I'll be able to communicate with my friends and with adults I've never met every second of every day. And by the way, I'll never look up from my hand again." They would have said no.

Or, maybe you'd try going to them and saying, "Now that I'm 12, I want to take 200 pictures of myself in a skimpy bikini and put them someplace where everyone in my school can see them and tell me if they like how I look." (A fairly accurate definition of Instagram.) Again, they would have said no.

Today, most parents say yes to these requests. Or they say yes without knowing what they're saying yes to when they hand their kids a smartphone. They're not bad parents—they're often the same parents who set rules for their kids in the real world. But with smartphones and social media, it's become very easy for parents and kids to get swept up in what everyone else is doing. And everyone *is* doing it: On average, kids now get their first smartphone around age 11, and 38% of 10- to 12-year-olds use social media. As you saw in the last chapter, the results have been catastrophic.

With use so pervasive and the dangers so dire, parents are in a tough spot. But there is a way out: You have to be in charge.

For a previous generation of parents, that was obvious (and if you didn't like it, well, sonny, you can get out of the car and walk). For us, it's not. Being an authority figure seems a little strange. We left behind the harmful practices of our parents and grandparents, like spanking and shaming. We vowed we would never say "because I said so." We want to show our kids we love them, and we don't want them to be upset. Is it working? Only sort of.

THE BEST PARENTING STYLE

Parenting styles are a favorite topic in popular media, so you may have heard of helicopter parenting (hovering over kids), snowplow parenting (removing all of the obstacles in their way), gentle parenting (never saying no), or lighthouse parenting (being a source for insight but not interfering too much).

Academic research has instead focused on four parenting styles. Each is low or high on affection and low or high on rules. It looks like this, with my addition of an ocean animal name for each, so they're easier to remember:

	Low affection	**High affection**
Low rules	Uninvolved (fish)	Permissive (sea sponge)
High rules	Authoritarian (tiger shark)	Authoritative (dolphin)

Figure 1.1: The four parenting styles

What does each of these mean in practice?

- **Uninvolved parenting (Fish parenting).** These parents provide for children's basic needs but then offer little nurturance or expectations. They are a little like fish, who lay eggs and then swim away, leaving their offspring to fend for themselves. Fish parents don't set rules but also don't show much affection or love.

- **Permissive parenting (Sea sponge parenting).** Sea sponges have no backbone, and neither do permissive parents. They are affectionate and nurturing, but don't set limits for their kids. Elsewhere I've seen them called jellyfish parents, but since jellyfish sting, this doesn't fit. Permissive parents have no sting. "Gentle parenting" is a type of permissive parenting—lots of affection but few rules and little enforcement.

- **Authoritarian parenting (Tiger shark parenting).** These parents enforce rigid rules, rarely explain anything, and punish harshly. They seldom show affection and aren't very nurturant. This is the old-school parent who answers questions with "because I said so." They're like the shark who goes straight for the bite. Authoritarian parenting overlaps with the "Tiger Mom" idea of expecting kids to obey so they can succeed in ways the parent deems important (such as getting all A's or making a sports team).

- **Authoritative parenting (Dolphin parenting).** This is the best of both worlds: a parent who shows affection but also sets boundaries and rules. That also means parents usually explain why the rules are there instead of resorting to "because I said so." The "dolphin" label comes from authoritative parents being firm but flexible, like the body of a dolphin. This analogy is admittedly what my kids call "cringe," but it's also memorable.

The research is clear that authoritative (dolphin) parenting works the best and leads to the most well-adjusted children, because it includes both affection and rules. The other parenting styles all fail in one way or another. Permissive (sea sponge) parenting sounds fun and loving, but doesn't work out well in the short term (kids who are never told no are often terrors) or the long term (what happens when they go to school or have a job and are told no?). Uninvolved (fish) parents are the worst of both worlds: They don't set rules or show affection. Both of these parenting styles set few limits on kids, which often leads to unhealthy choices (like Cocoa Puffs for dinner or staying up until midnight on a school night).

Tiger shark authoritarian parents set rules but end up with children who misbehave when they're left on their own without the parent there to enforce the rules. The children of tiger shark parents often develop into adults who need external pressure to get motivated. The parent-child relationship also suffers when parents don't show affection.

Authoritative (dolphin) parenting also works the best for device use. It means setting reasonable rules and enforcing them, while also being affectionate and empathetic to children's needs. Clinical psychologist and parenting expert Becky Kennedy calls this type of parenting "Sturdy Leadership"—it's a combination of validating feelings but also holding boundaries. She suggests parents should respond to kids pushing back on rules with something like this: "One of my main jobs is to make decisions that I think are good for you, even when you're upset with me. This is one of those times. I get that you're upset, I really do."

LONG-TERM GOALS

Most modern parents are on board with the validating feelings and empathy part of authoritative parenting. We want to show our kids we love them, and we empathize with our kids more than our parents did with us. We want our kids to be happy.

That's a good goal, but there's a difference between short-term happiness and long-term happiness. Your job is not to make your kids happy at every moment. It's to raise competent adults who will be happy in the long term. Your most important job as a parent is giving your children experiences that help them grow. Sure, there can be childish fun along the way, but not so much that it overwhelms healthy long-term development. That means having rules and enforcing them.

Parenting is different from other relationships: It is not a partnership of equals. Kids' brains aren't equipped to make the best choices for the future, so you have to guide them. Forget about always giving them what they want; give them what they need—not just for now but for the long term. That's the balance struck by authoritative (dolphin) parenting. Yes, we want to be close to our kids, but we're not their friends. We're their parents.

Thinking long-term, how can your child spend their time so they grow into a healthy, independent adult? More time on devices is not usually the answer to this question. The ultimate test is the opinions of young adults who grew up with these technologies. In a recent poll, half of 18- to 27-year-olds said they wished TikTok and Snapchat had never been invented. It is difficult to imagine that this many young adults in the 1990s wished TV was never invented. Nearly 6 out of 10 young adults think parents should not give children smartphones before high school. Activist groups like Design It For Us and LOG OFF, led by young adults, have lobbied Congress for more regulation of social media.

Even many kids are asking for more rules and less technology—this is not solely the province of parents and other older people. That should give you confidence in your decisions to limit your kids' device use. "Why do parents give their children smartphones?" asked middle school student Anushka Trivedi. "I think I finally know the answer now. Parents want to have a good relationship with their children, so they give them everything they want to make them happy." Her peers, she writes, "do not know how to control their smartphone usage. . . . When I look at my classmates' faces, absorbed in their smartphones, they look eerily expressionless, even hollow. Their eyes look tired and droopy; their faces look drained and sulking. They look like they have no choice."

When UK journalist Decca Aitkenhead asked sisters Edie, 15, and Rose, 13, if they loved social media, they looked at her like she was crazy. "You know it's all fake but you still feel like it's real. You still can't help comparing yourself with everyone who looks pretty and feeling bad about yourself," said Rose. When Aitkenhead asked the girls to join a group of teens giving up their phones for a month, they jumped at the chance. "It gives us an excuse," Edie said. "We get to escape this trap for a whole month without looking weird. We can say we're doing it for *The Sunday Times*."

Overall, kids are surprisingly self-aware that the time they spend online is often not beneficial or healthy. They've even come up with a name for the reality-bending effects of being chronically online: brain rot. The phrase is so descriptive of life today that the Oxford English Dictionary named it the word of the year for 2024.

WHY SETTING BOUNDARIES ON DEVICE USE IS HARD

Most parents figure out how to set reasonable limits in real-world contexts, like bedtimes and rules like "no dessert until you've finished your dinner." But with devices, setting boundaries often feels much harder. That's for at least four very understandable reasons:

1. **We didn't grow up with these technologies, so we often don't understand their pitfalls and dangers.** When you don't have an Instagram account, it's easy to optimistically assume that Instagram is just a place where teens share pictures with each other. Even if you have an Instagram account, your feed probably looks different from your kid's and has a different impact on you. When you have never heard of Discord, it's difficult to imagine that the platform has allowed adults to blackmail teens into attempting suicide (which, unfortunately, it has). When you didn't get a smartphone until you were an adult, it's difficult to imagine the teen requirement of instant responses to texts. Many of us don't realize just how easy it is for kids to access pornography online because when we were younger porn was much harder for kids to access.

2. **It's difficult to observe what kids are doing on their devices.** Unless you have the highest level of parental monitoring software installed, you probably have no idea what your kid is doing on their phone. When J does her homework on paper, I can see she's doing her homework. When she does it on her school laptop, I never know if she's doing homework or watching YouTube.

3. **There are few regulations in place to protect children online.** If your 13-year-old wants to drive a car, you can say no. You can tell them, truthfully, that the law requires that they be a minimum age (usually 16) and have a license, and that they (or you) could get arrested if they drove. If your kid wants to smoke cigarettes, you can tell them they won't be able to buy them until they are 18 or 21. If they want to drink alcohol, you can say they must be the minimum age for their county. In contrast, the few laws that exist for social media and websites are rarely enforced. The parent who doesn't want their kid to buy alcohol can usually count on the drinking age being enforced by bars, restaurants, and stores. The parent who doesn't want their kid to use social media is pretty much on their own. Yes, this is hard—but most worthwhile things are hard. And even setting some limits is better than none. That's where this book comes in—to help you set those boundaries.

4. **The consequences for kids breaking the rules are often unclear.** Fortunately, they don't have to be. Let's say a kid grabs their phone in the middle of the night to watch videos. What do you do—should you take their phone away

for a day or two? Some argue that this isn't a good solution because then they are cut off from their friends. But you could also argue that that makes the consequence even more impactful, and the incentive to follow the rules even more powerful. It also makes sense in the context of other activities. If a teen didn't follow the rules of driving—if, say, they got two speeding tickets in a month—nearly every parent would agree that they shouldn't be able to drive for a while. Having a phone is a privilege, not a right. If they can't use it responsibly, they can't use it at all for a few days.

If your kid really needs their phone outside the house, you can still take it away when they are at home. If they then decide they're going to spend all of their time away from home, you can restrict what the phone can do, using parental controls to cut off access to everything but calling and texting (third-party software is going to work best; see Rules 6 and 9). That also works if you don't want to physically take the phone from your kid.

The good news is most kids, even teens, respond to structure and limits. They like knowing what to expect and what the rules are, even around screens. When E started watching TV nearly all day on the weekends in 8th grade, I was tempted to let it go. I knew she was struggling with some friend issues at school and I didn't want to make her unhappy. But I realized that she was missing out on other things, like spending time with her sisters and reading, that would be better for her than hours of TV. I told her that from now on she could watch TV only after dinner. I took the TV remote and hid it.

Frankly, I expected a meltdown, but I didn't get one. At first she wasn't happy, but within a day she'd found other things to do; she and her younger sister started spending more time on their bikes and more time goofing around with each other. Some nights she doesn't even ask for the remote anymore. I think this worked because the rule was clear and there was no easy way to circumvent it—she had to get the remote from me.

HOW FLEXIBLE SHOULD YOU BE, AND HOW MUCH SHOULD YOU EXPLAIN?

Being in charge doesn't mean being completely inflexible. Sometimes your kids will have a good reason to use their phone on vacation, for example. Still, if you give in, it's harder to go back. An absolute rule is almost always easier to enforce than a piecemeal one. And although it's good to share your reasoning behind rules with your kids, too much explaining invites arguing back. It's a delicate balance.

Your level of flexibility and explanations will partially depend on the age of your children. For younger children—say, elementary school age—simple rules are best and not as much context is necessary. Tell them what the rule is, and if they ask why, explain it briefly. Most kids this age will accept the rule without much pushback.

By the time your kid is in middle school, though, you'll need to explain the rules in more detail. Tell them about how devices interfere with sleep (Rule 2) and about the downsides of social media (Rule 3). They still may argue, but you're more likely to get buy-in if you've told them why the rule is important. If they say all their friends have social media or a smartphone, say different families have different rules. After they hit middle school, it's also harder to enforce an absolute no-devices rule, because they will likely need to do at least some of their homework on a laptop. (There's more on laptops in Rule 9.)

If you have more than one child, you'll have to be ready to respond to "but my brother gets to . . ." if you have children of different ages. Tell your younger child they will also have the privilege when they reach that age. But being in charge and having some rules gives you a basic roadmap to navigate through each child's individual circumstances.

CONVERSATIONS TO HAVE WITH YOUR KIDS

Of course, it's not just explaining the rules—you'll also want to talk to your kids about how social media works and some of the dangers they may face online.

To repeat: Conversations about tech dangers *cannot take the place of having rules*. Some people say parents don't need to set rules around technology because we should just teach kids to "use their devices responsibly." How about we do both? Let's teach them about the pitfalls of devices while *also* having rules to ease them into the Wild West of the online world. I can't see someone arguing that we should just talk to kids about not smoking and then teach them to "use tobacco responsibly." Instead, we rightly have laws against kids buying cigarettes. Similarly, having conversations about responsible tech use is necessary but not sufficient.

Once your kids are old enough to get on the internet, even

with parental controls in place, there are a few conversations you need to have with them. Talk about these things by the time they are 10, or younger if they have a device (including a tablet or laptop) with internet access.

1. **Never, ever send someone a nude picture of yourself.** Never. Once it's out there it can go anywhere—the person that has it has the power to send it to anyone you know. Don't give anyone that power.

2. **Don't post anything on social media or online that you wouldn't want announced on a loudspeaker at school.** You might think of it as just being for your friends, but you never know who's going to see it. Someone could take a picture or a screenshot of it and it could go anywhere. Plus, anything you post on social media can stay there forever. Same goes for posting pictures of friends or classmates that might embarrass them. Don't do it.

3. **Don't share information about your identity online or while gaming.** That includes your home address, your Social Security number, and your passwords. If you get an email that sounds urgent, think twice before clicking on any links.

4. **Don't assume that texts or Snapchats are private.** Texts feel private because they're usually exchanged between two people, but if the friendship goes sour—as can happen, especially among kids—those texts could be used as ammunition. Snapchats can be screenshotted and posted.

Set social media accounts to private, but don't assume they will stay 100% private.

5. **Think twice, and three times, before you post anything mean, and then don't do it.** Imagine that you are saying it to their face. It's easy to dash off a cruel text or comment when someone isn't there in front of you, and harder to do it when you see the look on their face. But it will affect them just the same.

6. **If you're curious about bodies or sex, ask me first, or we can look it up together.** I've told my kids this many times and usually add this: If you go searching yourself, you might see things you can't unsee. There's just too much disturbing stuff online when you search for these topics. If you've installed parental controls that filter websites (see Rules 6 and 9), most sexually explicit material will be blocked, but stuff can sometimes get through. Some kids are open to the idea of coming to their parents with these types of questions. Others may be more reluctant, but it's good for them to know the offer is there.

7. **Your time is a precious resource.** Ask your teens this question: What are you going to remember from your teen years—the hours you spent playing *Block Blast*, or the times you spent with your friends in person? What could you get better at—reading, drawing, playing the guitar—if you stopped scrolling Instagram? Some kids will argue that they explore their interests through social media. That may be true, but they are also well aware it's a huge time sink.

Teach them that moderation is key—and then put the parental controls (see Rule 6) in place to make sure you're not wasting your breath. This is definitely a situation where talking isn't enough.

BE A ROLE MODEL

Last but not least: Put your own phone away as much as you can. It's usually not a good idea to say one thing and do another. Being a good role model is important—teens in particular can smell hypocrisy miles away. If you hate it when your kids pull out their phones during a conversation, you shouldn't be doing that either. As the adult, you are allowed a certain amount of "digital hypocrisy"—you may need to be glued to your phone sometimes if you're on call at work or are the contact for an elderly parent. But as much as possible, model the tech behavior you'd like to see.

COMMON OBSTACLES AND PUSHBACKS

1. **"You can't put the genie back in the bottle."** I sometimes hear this from parents who have already given their kids a smartphone or let them use social media. But of course you can go back—remember, you're in charge. It's never too late, and the best time to change is right now. Set the smartphone aside until they are older and, if they really need a phone, get them a basic phone (see Rule 4). Uninstall the problematic social media app or set time limits on it (see Rule 6). Becky Kennedy advises parents to think of themselves as a pilot "who always has the right to return to

base should the skies be more turbulent than expected—in fact, this is something the passengers would want a pilot to do, even if they seem annoyed in the moment. You are the pilot of your family plane."

2. **"But Mom/Dad, all of my friends . . . [have a gaming console in their bedroom/are on Snapchat/have a smartphone]."** Remember what your parents said when you made this argument? "If all of your friends jumped off a cliff, would you?" You might have been arguing about dying your hair, getting a belly button piercing, collecting as many Beanie Babies as your friends, or staying out until midnight. Sure, sometimes your parents said yes, but just as often they said no, and they usually weren't particularly persuaded by the "everyone's doing it" idea. You shouldn't be either. Devices aren't any different. Your kids will still find ways to keep in touch with their friends.

3. **"You're ruining my life!"** Ah, the age-old teen lament. College students whose parents put restrictions on their devices when they were younger always tell me they're glad their parents did so. Others tell me about the negative—and occasionally horrifying—experiences they had on social media, sometimes at extremely young ages. In other words, you're not ruining your kid's life by setting some boundaries around devices. You're improving it.

RULE 2: NO ELECTRONIC DEVICES IN THE BEDROOM OVERNIGHT

When Diana Park's daughter was in 7th grade, she got her first smartphone. The middle-schooler knew she was not supposed to be on her phone after bedtime. But then, late one night, Diana heard her daughter talking and went to investigate. Her 12-year-old was FaceTiming with a friend at midnight—a good three hours after her bedtime. The girl then confessed that her siblings did the same.

Diana's kids are not alone. A shocking 6 out of 10 kids used their phones between midnight and 5 a.m. on school nights in a study that tracked 11- to 17-year-olds' phone use for a week. Some kids delay going to sleep because it's too difficult to put down their phones. Others wake up in the middle of the night and can't resist grabbing it. "Sometimes I look up and it's 3 a.m. and I'm watching a video of a giraffe eating a steak," said 15-year-old Owen Lanahan. "And I wonder, 'How did I get here?'"

"How did we get here?" is a good question. An even better one is "How can we get out?"

And it is imperative that we do. Not getting enough sleep is a risk factor for just about everything we'd like our kids to avoid, from getting sick to feeling depressed. Yet most kids—90% according to one study—are not getting enough sleep. And if they are waking up in the middle of the night to use their phones, as a third of teens admitted to in one survey, the sleep they do get is fragmented and low quality.

HOW MUCH SLEEP DO KIDS AND TEENS NEED?

Kids and teens need more sleep than you might think—see Figure 2.1 for how much sleep your kids should be getting based on their age.

Age group	Average amount of sleep needed per day
Infants	14 hours
Toddlers (ages 1–2)	12.5 hours
Preschoolers (3–5)	11.5 hours
Elementary age children (6–12)	11 hours
Teens (13–17)	9 hours
Adults (18+)	8 hours

Figure 2.1: Recommended amount of daily sleep by age group

Note: Averages based on the National Sleep Foundation recommended ranges for daily sleep needs in each age group.

For most people, the biggest surprise is that teens need more sleep than adults do, not less—about nine hours a night. And while tweens (ages 10 to 12) don't need as much sleep as six-year-olds, most still need nine and a half or 10 hours of sleep.

Getting younger children to go to bed on time can be difficult enough, but once kids start puberty it's often even harder. Puberty shifts the brain's sleep-wake cycle later so it's hard to fall asleep early. Combine that with early school start times, and kids often need to go to bed before they naturally feel tired. An 11-year-old who needs to get up by 6:30 a.m. to catch a 7 a.m. school bus needs to be asleep—not just in bed—by 9 p.m. to get enough sleep. A 15-year-old on this schedule needs to be asleep by 9:30 p.m.

WHY BEDTIMES ARE IMPORTANT

So, before we even think about electronic devices, the first thing you need to do is this:

Set a bedtime for your kid and stick to it as much as possible. Partially due to the later circadian rhythm during puberty, 10- to 15-year-olds need a bedtime just as much or more than younger children. When parents enforce bedtimes, studies find teens get nearly a half hour more sleep—that adds up to three and a half hours more sleep a week. Teens whose parents let them stay up until midnight were 24% more likely to suffer from depression and 20% more likely to have suicidal thoughts than those whose parents had set a bedtime of 10 p.m. or earlier.

Even on weekends when your kids don't need to be up early for school, they should still have a bedtime—preferably the same bedtime as on weekdays. Both adults and kids sleep better when they go to bed and get up at the same time each day. It's unlikely your teens are going to be up at 7 a.m. on Saturday morning, but if they have gone to sleep near bedtime the night before they're much less likely to sleep until noon. They are also more likely to make up some of the sleep they missed during the school week if they go to bed on time.

There will of course be exceptions to bedtimes, but these should be fairly rare—once a month or less, not once a week: think vacations, dances, and sleepovers, not every weekend night. Even older teens will quickly wear themselves down if they're regularly staying out late on the weekends and then getting up early for school on the weekdays. Some kids will fight bedtimes, but if their devices aren't in their bedrooms—as we'll soon cover—they are often much more willing to go to bed. It also helps to be consistent. My kids have argued with me over many things, but they have rarely fought me over bedtimes because they knew they wouldn't get anywhere. It's one thing I never compromised on.

How old do teens need to be before they don't have a bedtime anymore? That depends not just on age but on their behavior and maturity. One fall when daylight savings kicked in, my kids asked me what their new bedtimes were given the time change. I told our younger two children their bedtimes and then thought for a minute about our oldest, who was 16, very independent, and had voluntarily put herself on an early schedule. "K, you can decide your own bedtime," I said. There was a moment of stunned silence and then she said, "I've been waiting for you to say that my entire life." Maybe, but she had to earn it to hear it. And if she'd started staying up too late on school nights, a bedtime would have been back.

As a general rule, choose a bedtime 15 to 30 minutes earlier than your kids need to be asleep. It takes most people 15 to 30 minutes to fall asleep after getting in bed and turning the lights out. Setting a slightly earlier bedtime than absolutely necessary is also a useful psychological trick. If your 12-year-old needs to be asleep by 9:30 p.m. and their bedtime is 9:00, they will feel like they're getting away with something if they get in bed at 9:15 on occasion—and they'll still be getting enough sleep.

AVOIDING THE SCREEN MONSTERS

Once you've set your kids' bedtime, you're ready to make the rule: *No devices in the bedroom overnight.* That means not just no phones, tablets, or laptops, but also no TVs or gaming consoles in your kid's bedroom. Decades of research have found that kids who have a TV or gaming console in their room don't sleep enough. These devices don't belong in kids' bedrooms.

Getting devices physically out of the bedroom after lights-out prevents three sleep-disturbing monsters:

1. **The *I Might as Well See What's Going on Monster*: Using the device in the middle of the night or being awakened by it.** Recall that six out of 10 teens use their phones between midnight and 5 a.m. on school nights at least once a week. That's not just from staying up late—28% of 12- and 13-year-olds used their phones when they woke up during the night. One out of four said that texts or phone calls

had woken them up after they went to sleep. If the device is in the bedroom, it's very tempting to see if your friend texted you back, how many likes you've gotten on your social media post, or what new videos have shown up. And if the ringer is left on, the automatic response is to look at the phone to see what's going on. With the device in the bedroom, kids will wake up multiple times a night and then have to try to go back to sleep. With so many kids using their phones at night, at least one of their friends is probably awake, too.

2. **The *Just One More Video Monster*: Delaying going to bed because they want to keep using the device.** Middle and high school kids are already predisposed to stay up late due to the shift in their circadian rhythm. Throw in the siren song of videos, texting friends, and the endless scroll of social media and it's all over. And if there's a gaming console in the room? Forget about it.

3. **The *Ha! Try to Sleep Now! Monster*: Using the device in bed right before going to sleep.** This is a problem even if it's not kids' bedtime yet, for three reasons. First, nearly everything kids do on their devices is psychologically stimulating, so devices rev up the brain when it should be slowing down. Second, they are learning to associate their bed with stimulation rather than rest. So even on nights when they don't use a device in bed, they've conditioned their brain to expect stimulation there, and they'll have a harder time falling asleep. Third, the blue light from devices tricks the brain into thinking it's still daytime. Then they don't

produce enough of the sleep hormone melatonin, and it takes longer to fall asleep and is more difficult to sleep soundly. And if the device is in bed with them right before bedtime, it's more likely to stay there overnight—cue Monster #1.

This is why study after study has found that kids who have access to their devices in their bedrooms do not sleep as well or for as long. Kids who used their devices right before sleep, compared to those who didn't, were 44% more likely to not sleep enough and 51% more likely to not sleep well in an analysis of 20 studies (see Figure 2.2). In another study, 11- to 14-year-olds slept nearly a half hour less on nights when they texted or played games on a device while in bed before they went to sleep. Kids who used their devices before sleep were also more likely to feel sleepy during the day. Just having *access*

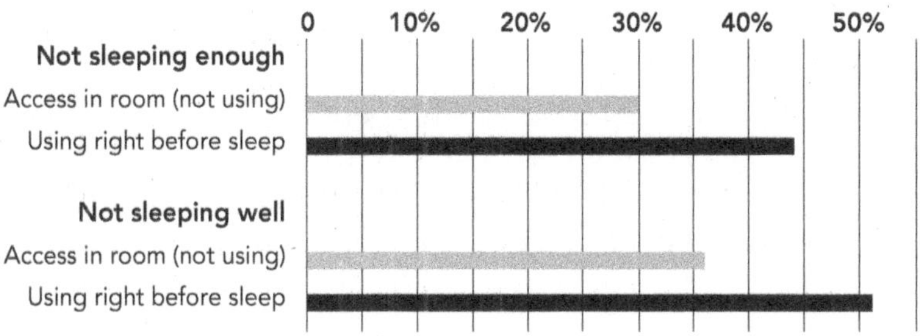

Figure 2.2: Risk of not sleeping enough and not sleeping well by access and use of devices in the bedroom, 6- to 18-year-olds

Source: Carter et al. (2016)

Note: "Not sleeping enough" means inadequate sleep hours (nine or fewer hours for children, eight or fewer hours for teens). "Not sleeping well" means poor sleep quality (trouble falling asleep, non-refreshing sleep, waking up too often).

to the device in the room, even if it wasn't used, was linked to not sleeping enough and not sleeping well.

Some kids will argue that they should be able to have their devices in their room overnight because they will turn them off before they go to sleep. This data suggests that's not a good idea. Plus, how do you know if they have actually turned it off and kept if off? You don't, because, with any luck, you're asleep.

By the way, the no devices in the bedroom overnight rule applies to adults as well. You will sleep better if you put your phone, tablet, and laptop outside your bedroom. You may need to be guilty of digital hypocrisy sometimes, but you should follow this rule yourself if at all possible.

PUTTING THE RULES IN MOTION

With all this in mind, you're ready to take the two steps necessary to protect your kids' sleep from devices:

Step #1: Make it a house rule that devices must be outside kids' bedrooms after bedtime.

Step #2: Use the parental controls on your kid's device to shut it down at bedtime.

Families have a number of ways of implementing Step #1. Here are a few possibilities:

A. **Everyone puts their devices on the charging station away from the bedrooms before bed.** You'll need to check that your kids' devices are there before they go to bed. Most families put the charging station in the kitchen. As a bonus, kids' devices will be fully charged in the morning before they go to school.

B. **Devices go in a lockbox overnight.** Go this route if you're concerned your kid will sneak into the kitchen to get their phone in the middle of the night. There are three styles of lockboxes. The most sophisticated is a lockbox with a timer—one brand is called a kSafe (short for kitchen safe). Phones go in the kSafe and are accessible only when the timer runs out at the specified time in the morning. The second type opens with a key. Hide the key in your bedroom. The downside is you might lose it, especially if you move the location to keep the kids off the trail. The third option is a clear lockbox with a three-digit combination, since it's more convenient than repeatedly hiding a key. (These lockboxes are also good for other purposes, like storing Girl Scout cookies or other foods that tend to mysteriously disappear from the pantry while every child denies it was them. We have six.)

C. **Kids hand you their phones when they go to bed, and you keep them in your bedroom.** They then get them back before they leave for school. This is a secure method but only works if you go to bed later than your children (or your spouse does) and one of you is always awake and at home when your kids leave for school.

Step #2 is using parental controls. Parental control dashboards have a setting that allows parents to restrict the hours when the phone can be used. During those hours, the device automatically shuts off (or can be used only for essential functions like calling), and it can't be used again until the window opens back up in the morning. I suggest having the phone and laptop shut off a half hour before bedtime. We'll cover how to use parental controls in Rule 6.

It might be tempting to only do one of these steps, but both are necessary. If you do #2 (parental controls) and not #1 (no devices in the bedroom) there are still costs for sleep, given the research showing sleep is disrupted by devices in the bedroom even if kids aren't using them. Plus, some kids have found ways around parental controls, especially if they have smartphones instead of basic phones.

If you do #1 (no devices in the bedroom) and not #2 (parental controls), your kid might still end up on their device in the middle of the night if routines are disrupted, parents forget to make sure the phones are where they are supposed to be, or kids are sneaky.

It happens. One night I glanced at the kitchen counter and saw that J's phone was there before I put her to bed. A few minutes later I realized I'd forgotten something downstairs and looked at the kitchen counter again. J's phone wasn't there. I wondered if my memory was playing tricks on me. I cracked open J's bedroom door and asked her where her phone was. "It's not downstairs?" she said, seemingly surprised. She said she didn't know where her phone was and we spent the next half hour looking for it. When I told E what I was doing, she immediately said, "It's in her bed." Sure enough, it was—J had snuck downstairs, grabbed the phone, run upstairs, and put the phone in her bed. Apparently she'd been doing this on and off for weeks—and this was a child who rarely lied. Because the parental controls shut down her phone after bedtime, she couldn't use it in the middle of the night. She claimed she put the phone in her bed so she could listen to podcasts as soon as she woke up. I told her she had to go get her phone downstairs in the morning if she wanted to do that, and I took her phone away for three days.

COMMON OBSTACLES AND PUSHBACKS

1. **"But I have to have my phone in my bedroom overnight. It's my alarm clock."** I have some advice for you: Buy an alarm clock. This goes for adults as well as kids. If you're concerned about power outages, buy a battery-operated alarm clock. Even better, have one alarm clock that plugs in and another one running on batteries, and set both. You can buy the alarm clock online on your phone—and then put your phone away and get a good night's sleep.

2. **"I have to stay up late (on my device) because I need to finish my homework."** Especially if kids get home late from sports practice or other activities, that is sometimes true. However, this dilemma is often due to procrastination and not managing time well. Start there. Advise them to try to finish their work ahead of deadlines when they know they'll be busy with other things later (this is a great strategy for college and adult life as well).

   Also let them know that sports and homework don't seem to be the primary causes of not getting enough sleep—

screen activities are. Eighth graders who participate in sports or who go out with their friends are actually *less* likely to be short on sleep, and homework time isn't linked with sleep in either direction (see Figure 2.3). The other pattern that's immediately noticeable: All of the screen activities (like gaming and social media) are linked to getting less sleep, and all of the non-screen activities (like sports and getting together with friends) are linked to more sleep.

3. **"I forgot."** What if your kids say "I forgot to put it on the charging station" or say they put their phone downstairs when it's actually in their bed, like J did? Then they lose the privilege of having the phone during the day for one day (for "I forgot") or three days (if they lie or try to sneak the phone in).

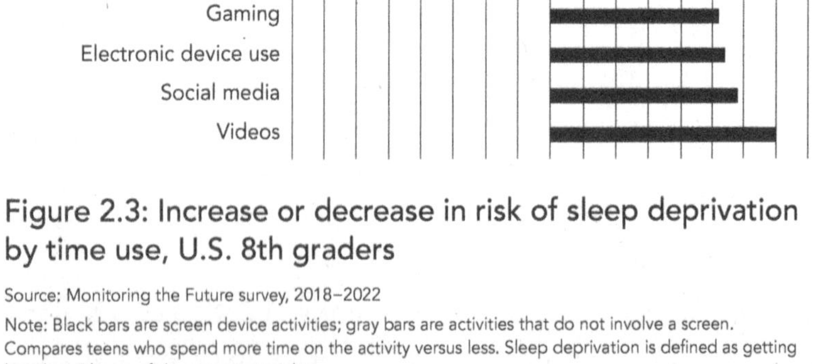

Figure 2.3: Increase or decrease in risk of sleep deprivation by time use, U.S. 8th graders

Source: Monitoring the Future survey, 2018–2022

Note: Black bars are screen device activities; gray bars are activities that do not involve a screen. Compares teens who spend more time on the activity versus less. Sleep deprivation is defined as getting less than 7 hours of sleep on most nights.

4. **"I can't find my phone—that's why it's not on the charging station."** E tried this. I told her it was her responsibility to keep track of where her phone was, or she wasn't ready for a phone and I would take it away or get her a flip phone. She miraculously found her phone.

5. **"But my friend really needs me right now."** If your kid's friend really needs them that much after bedtime, they probably need help from an adult. Teen girls—and sometimes boys as well—can fall into the role of 24/7 unpaid therapist for their friends. It's not only stressful but leads to not getting enough sleep. They can talk or text with their friend until a half hour before bedtime, but at that point they need to suggest their friend talk to their parents or contact a mental health helpline.

If you have the bandwidth to fully follow only one rule in this book, make it this one. No devices in the bedroom overnight is very straightforward and costs nothing. The research is very clear that devices interfere with sleep, and sleep is absolutely crucial for both physical and mental health. When my daughters were babies, my favorite book on child sleep was titled *Healthy Sleep Habits, Happy Child*. That sums it up just as well for teens as it does for infants. With sleep so vitally important, we can't let technology get in the way.

RULE 3: NO SOCIAL MEDIA UNTIL AGE 16—OR LATER

"Half of my friends have an eating disorder from TikTok, and the other half are lying," a teen girl told filmmaker Lauren Greenfield. "Social media makes a lot of teens feel like crap but they don't know how to stop using it," said another. A third said, "It is so scary that we are allowed to actually do this."

The truth is they shouldn't be. But because social media is virtually unregulated, it's up to parents to keep their kids off the apps. It's become common for 10- and 11-year-olds to use TikTok and Snapchat, even though the current minimum age for social media is 13.

Even if age were verified, 13 is far too low. Thirteen was not chosen for any developmental or social reason; it was a compromise politicians reached with tech companies in 1998 at the dawn of the internet. But what parent or educator has ever said, "Right during early puberty—wow, that sounds like the perfect time to introduce social media!"? Needless to say, it's not. In fact, developmentally, it's the worst time, right as middle school kids' brains become hyper-attuned to social status and reward-seeking.

It's also not a great time for solid judgment. Younger teens have more trouble controlling their impulses than older teens and young adults, partially due to the activation of the adolescent brain: The limbic (emotional) system is on high alert, the prefrontal cortex (self-control) is less developed, and the two areas do not communicate as well as they do in adults.

By law, we protect 13- to 15-year-olds from just about everything adult in the physical world, from cigarettes to alcohol to driving, because we know they are not ready for it. They are also not ready for social media.

As an age to start using social media, 16 is a compromise. We trust kids to start driving at 16—not a magic number, but one society has agreed upon as a milestone for maturity. Sixteen is beyond the middle school and early high school years when puberty and awkwardness are at their peak. Kids mature a lot from 13 to 16. Some 16-year-olds may not be ready for social media either, but others may want to get involved in politics or community groups using social media. I have made the rule "age 16 or later" for this reason, but if you want to make it 18 for your kids, that's even better. (And I know some who want to make it 30. You can try, but good luck.)

Eighteen, the age of legal adulthood, actually does make some sense given the agreements users must accept when opening a social media account. What other contract can minors sign other than those allowing social media apps access to their personal data? Even 17-year-olds are required to get a parent signature just to go on a school field trip.

That said, 16 versus 18 is a minor disagreement when 68% of 11- and 12-year-olds—none of whom are legally allowed to have accounts—freely admit to using social media like Instagram and Snapchat. For kids 15 and under, the risks of social media clearly outweigh any possible benefits. In a 2024 poll, three out of four parents said they regretted letting their kids access social media.

WHAT'S SO BAD ABOUT SOCIAL MEDIA?

There are many reasons children and younger teens should not use social media. I'll share a few of the most important in this section. Not every kid will have these experiences, but many will, with consequences from the merely upsetting to the tragic. Because we didn't grow up with these platforms, most parents have no idea this type of darkness exists on social media. I didn't know either until I started doing in-depth research in the area. A warning: Some of this is disturbing, but I share it to strengthen your resolve to say no when your kids ask for social media, and to (selectively) share with them if they ask why you're saying no. Buckle up.

- **Contact from unknown adults.** Adults can easily message minors on social media apps and solicit them for nude pictures or ask to meet. At E's 14th birthday party, I was grabbing a bite to eat in the kitchen when I overheard one of her friends (I'll call her Kylie) say, "Then he asked me where I was and what I was wearing. I told him, 'Dude, I'm on the middle school bus!'" I found out the rest of the story later: A man Kylie didn't know had messaged her on Instagram and was hitting on her.

This is common: One in five 13- to 15-year-old girls have been sexually propositioned via social media. Even more, 37%, report being exposed to unwanted nudity. The majority of teen girls who use Instagram or Snapchat have been contacted on the app by a stranger who made them uncomfortable.

- **Sextortion.** Scammers target teens to extort money from them, usually through some form of blackmail. An extorter will often pose as someone close in age who's romantically interested, gaining a young person's trust through continued messages. They will then ask a kid or teen to share nude pictures or videos of themselves. Once they have a photo showing the child's face as well as their genitals, the blackmail begins. The sextortionist threatens to send the pictures to the teen's friends and family unless the kid pays hundreds of dollars. This happens to both boys and girls. In recent years, Snapchat alone has received more than 10,000 reports of sextortion a *month*, which their own internal analysis concluded "likely represent(s) a small fraction of this abuse."

- **Harmful content.** Some social media accounts promote eating disorders, such as "pro-ana" (meaning pro-anorexia) content. Others teach techniques for self-harm and even suicide, glorifying cutting and death. When a U.S. senator's staffers opened a test account on Instagram as a 13-year-old girl, searches for posts on healthy eating quickly led to a feed filled with pro-anorexia accounts and posts promoting self-harm. Once a kid starts looking at harmful posts or videos, perhaps during a passing bad mood, the algorithm learns to serve them up more. This can happen if they unconsciously linger over disturbing content a second longer than usual. Not all kids' accounts turn negative, but it's more likely to happen among those who are already more vulnerable. About half of young adults say they've seen at least one self-harm post on Instagram, and a shocking one out of three of those copied the behavior and harmed themselves in the same way.

UK teen Molly Russell's Instagram delivered more than 300 posts a month related to suicide, self-harm, and depression before she took her own life at the age of 14. Instead of classifying her death as a suicide, the coroner wrote that she "died from an act of self-harm while suffering from depression and the negative effects of online content." A child psychiatrist who examined Molly's feed said it was so disturbing he found it difficult to sleep for several weeks.

Teens can also find this type of material through a Google search, but in that case they have to go looking for it. Social media feeds it to them through an algorithm beyond their control. One study found that users struggling with eating disorders (versus those who were not) were shown 146% more appearance-oriented videos, 335% more diet-related videos, and 4343% more toxic eating disorder videos on TikTok.

Aren't social media companies supposed to remove this type of content? They are, but they don't seem to be trying very hard. Danish researchers created fake Instagram profiles that shared self-harm content. Even as the accounts displayed razor blades and blood, not a single image was removed from the site. When they created their own simple AI tool to analyze the content, it flagged 88% of the most severe images. The researchers concluded that Instagram has the technology available to take down most of this content but "has chosen not to implement it effectively."

- **Disturbing content.** Social media algorithms often serve up disturbing material because users tend to look at it longer—even if they would rather look away. Jamie, a student in my college class, used to love watching funny cat videos on social media. "How could I not? They are so fluffy!" he wrote. "Now, however, I frequently receive heartbreaking videos of cats in critical condition on Instagram Reels. There they are injured, distressed, and in pain. I hesitate to swipe because it hurts to see that and it feels even worse to have the ability to just 'move on' and do nothing." Social media, he says, often "takes something good or enjoyable and turns it negative."

  The TikTok feed of Chase Nasca, 16, grew increasingly dark in the early days of 2022, including a video of a man walking toward an oncoming train. Five days later, Chase deliberately walked into the path of a train and was killed. A year after his death, his TikTok feed was still playing videos glorifying suicide, including one that said, "Take the pain away. Death is a gift." TikTok had still not taken down the posts.

- **Competition for likes and followers.** Popularity can now be quantified: How many followers do you have? How many likes did you get on your post? Many teens say waiting for the likes to come in on a post is very anxiety-provoking. Plus, only certain content gets likes—and it's not the type of content you probably want your teens to value (see the next point).

- **Sexualization of girls and women.** On social media, sex sells and skin gets likes. The girls interviewed in *Social Studies*, a documentary about social media use, mentioned this often. Jordan, 15, says, "Nobody really slides up on your story unless you post something, like, really revealing. . . . If you post your face, they'll just kind of like go past it. But if you like, post your boobs with it they'll be like 'oh my God you look so good!'" This calculus of skin for likes skews what girls share and what they value. Sydney, 18, said, "A lot of us don't post about our passions because I've posted pictures, photography pictures I've taken, even sunset pictures, those get zero likes."

- **Cyberbullying and drama.** Even adults post cruel things on social media they would never say to someone's face. Then add in the high emotions and low self-control of the adolescent years, plus first forays into dating and sexuality, and things are primed to explode. In *Social Studies*, Bella, 16, says she and another girl both liked the same boy. The girl, she says, "filmed me sitting with all the boys [and said] I want to sleep with all the guys. . . . Her number one name was 'slut' and 'whore.'" Dominic, 17, was on the receiving end of hateful comments on his social media posts. "Because I'm Brown and I'm a bigger person, I guess you could call me a cyberbully's field day," he said. "I was missing days of school; I was not ever able to get out of bed. I was in this constant state of torture."

- **The time sink.** The algorithms of social media are designed to "maximize engagement." That means keeping users on for as long as possible and coming back as often as possible.

Kids (and adults, too) often mean to open a social media app and stay on it for a few minutes but end up spending much more time than they intended. Then they don't have as much time to do their homework, read, talk to friends in real time, go outside, or exercise.

This is the perfect fact to share with kids and teens: Tech companies make more money the longer users spend on the app and the more often they return. Social media apps are "free" because users don't pay with money—but they are not free, because you pay with your time, and your time is your life. Ask teens who they think invented the Snapstreak. Of course, it wasn't a fellow teen—it was a guy in Silicon Valley who wanted his bonus. (And probably got it and bought a Tesla.) Live your own life instead of funding a tech bro's Tesla.

And what do tech executives do with their own kids? Apple founder Steve Jobs didn't let his kids use the iPad. Bill Gates didn't give his kids smartphones until they were in high school and limited the amount of time his kids spent on devices. One of the most popular private schools in Silicon Valley is the Waldorf School, which doesn't include devices in the curriculum until high school and even then uses them sparingly. Tech executives seem to be following the rule of drug dealers, at least for their kids: Never get high on your own supply.

- **Social comparison.** Everyone else's life looks more glamorous on Instagram. Beginning in late childhood, kids start to compare themselves to others. That's natural, but social media gives them a distorted picture because most posts only highlight the positive. Even if a teen knows intellectually that a photo is retouched, it still feels bad to see so many perfect bodies and compare yourself. This is probably why social media use is linked to body image issues. Instagram parent company Meta's own research describes the "grief spiral" teen girls go through when they compare themselves to others on the platform, starting with insecurity and then moving on to bargaining, anger, withdrawal, and depression.

Alexa Mendes, now a college student, got accounts on Instagram and Snapchat when she was in 5th grade. By middle school, she began to realize they were making her feel bad about herself. "I never felt like I looked good enough in my photos. Then I would look at everyone else's feeds and they would seem like models in a photoshoot," she noted in her book *#Unsubscribed*, which she wrote when she was 16. "I was playing this comparison game, [which] was completely rigged. I was always comparing my entire life (problems, insecurities, weaknesses) with everyone else's highlight reel."

- **Mental health issues.** The connection between heavy social media use and mental health issues is strongest for children and younger teens, especially for girls. In a study of social media use and life satisfaction among teens in the UK, the strongest associations were for girls between the ages of 12 and 15. Figure 3.1 on the following page shows the stronger link between social media use and low life satisfaction for girls at age 14 compared to the weaker link at age 17. For boys, the connection between heavy social media use and

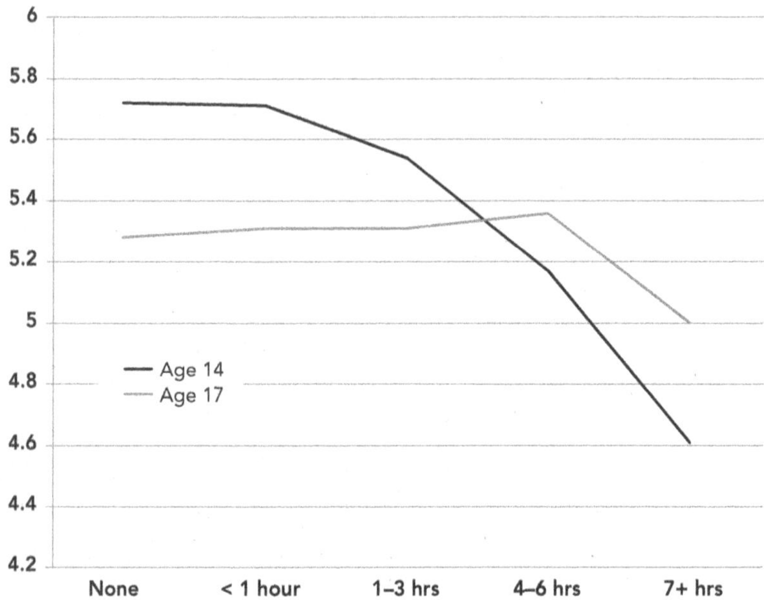

Figure 3.1: Hours of daily social media use and life satisfaction among UK girls, age 14 or age 17

Source: Orben et al. (2022)

low life satisfaction was worst around age 15. The authors of the study concluded that there are "developmental windows of sensitivity" to social media. In other words, social media is worse for the mental health of younger teens than for older ones.

"I got my first social media account, Instagram, in freshman year of high school," Olivia, a 20-year-old college student, told me. The apps were fun at first, but then "I constantly compared myself to other people. . . . I would feel my mental health and self-esteem fluctuate, which became exhausting. The internet quickly became a constant trigger of self-deterioration, anxiety, and depression. These apps, specifically TikTok, affected my attention span and schoolwork." Olivia eventually decided to delete the apps during her senior year of high school. She now describes herself as "two years TikTok sober"—a phrase of her own invention to describe breaking free of social media addiction.

WHAT TO ALLOW, AND WHAT NOT TO

There's no one definition of social media, and the popularity of apps changes quickly. Problematic platforms usually have features such as (1) algorithms, streaks, or push notifications creating compulsive or addictive use, (2) "likes" and followers creating competition, (3) short form videos, (4) endless scrolling (where there's not a natural end), and (5) problematic content or the ability for unknown adults to contact minors.

Here are my recommendations for which apps kids should not have before 16 and which you might consider letting them use at 15 and younger (though with limits). Some of these stories involve extreme outcomes, but they're the tip of the iceberg for the trouble, big and small, that kids can get into on social media. And just as in the previous section, some of what follows is disturbing.

THE NO LIST

- **Instagram.** With endless posts of perfect bodies and competition for likes and followers, Instagram should be off the table for under-16s. Notifications frequently draw users back to the app even when they want to take a break.

"Teens . . . often feel 'addicted' and know that what they're seeing is bad for their mental health but feel unable to stop themselves," concluded Meta's internal research on Instagram. Meta found that the platform made body image issues worse for one in three teen girls. Academic research has also linked Instagram to eating disorders and body image issues. The Instagram Stories feature has content that disappears after 24 hours, creating the fear of missing out (known as FOMO). Nearly 6 out of 10 people—including Instagram users themselves—said they would prefer to live in a world without Instagram.

When a researcher set up fake Instagram accounts giving an age of 13, Instagram Reels—the app's short video feed—showed a mix of videos, some with racy content such as women dancing seductively or posing to emphasize their breasts. When the accounts watched the racy videos, the app began to show videos with more explicit content, including those posted by adult content creators. After 20 minutes of watching Reels, the accounts' feeds filled with ads from sex content creators, including some who offered to send nude photos. In a later test, an account in the name of a 13-year-old was served numerous videos about anal sex within a half hour of joining the app. Meta's internal research found that teens saw three times as many posts with nudity, four times more bullying content, and nearly twice as much violence as adults 30 and over.

Instagram's Explore Page can suggest harmful content, especially influencers promoting starvation diets and posts featuring self-harm and suicide. Meta's internal research found that 13% of British teen users and 6% of American teen users who had suicidal thoughts said their desire to kill themselves traced back to Instagram. The app fed Englyn Roberts, 14, a post of a woman who screamed and pretended to hang herself with an electrical cord. Englyn fatally hung herself the same way. Her family is now suing Meta.

- **TikTok.** TikTok is known for having the most addictive algorithm out there. A third of teens say they use it "almost constantly." The "For You" page shows users what they think they want to see because it's designed to keep them on the app for as long as possible. Kids who intend to spend 15 minutes on the app often look up to find an hour or more has passed. On app stores, kids post reviews of TikTok saying things like "Do not download this app unless you're able to spend at least two hours a day on it. It's addicting!" and "I have some problems. My sister and brother and me are stuck at 3am scrolling through it!"

  TikTok is also an easy no because kids don't usually use it to communicate with each other, and everyone's feed is different. E once said she wanted TikTok so she could understand what her friends were talking about—but that argument doesn't hold water since feeds are individualized. When I mentioned that, she stopped asking.

  TikTok can send people down "black holes" of negative content if they use it when they are sad or anxious. They see a few videos about depression, and before long the app is serving up content about self-harm and suicide. Like Instagram, TikTok can also lead to negative comparisons. "When I'm on social media, it makes me feel so much smaller than I actually am. On TikTok, I'd see prettier girls than me and it would make me more upset," said 13-year-old Caylie.

Sexual content and drug content often slip by moderators. TikTok's internal research concluded that 100% of content "fetishizing minors" leaked through its moderation process, as did half of content glorifying the sexual assault of minors. When *The Wall Street Journal* created fake accounts on TikTok for 13-year-olds, they were almost immediately shown videos about drug use and paid pornography sites. A TikTok spokesperson told the *Journal* that the app doesn't filter feeds to minors—they get the same videos as adults. Apple told TikTok to rate the app as 17+ on the App Store, but TikTok refused and kept it listed as 12+.

TikTok has also been home to dangerous "challenges" like the Blackout challenge, where kids choke themselves, usually with a belt or leash, until they black out. The Blackout challenge has led to the deaths of at least 20 children, including 9- and 10-year-olds. The Chroming challenge, which involves inhaling toxic fumes from paint cans, gasoline, or nail polish remover, has also led to several deaths. The Skullbreaker challenge encourages kids to trick someone into jumping and then kicking their legs out from under them so they fall on their head. The Devious Licks challenge led to students destroying school property across the country.

- **Snapchat.** Snapchat users send each other "snaps" that disappear after a few seconds. Kids and teens like it because, ostensibly, there's not a permanent record of their silly facial expression or their face with puppy ears—or their nude picture. Unfortunately, there can be—it's possible to screenshot snaps (which, as one teen girl told me, are "good for blackmail"). Many parents assume teens only connect with friends on Snapchat, but the app also has a Quick Add feature that suggests new "friends" nearby and a Discovery feed with promoted content. It also has a "My Eyes Only" folder where kids can hide images they don't want their parents to see.

Snapchat doesn't have algorithms per se, but it does have Snapscores, which show how active users are on the platform. Snapscores increase the more friends you connect with, including those suggested through Quick Add. It also has Snapstreaks, the number of days two users have snapped each other—a supposed measure of the strength of a friendship. When I ask middle and high school students how many do Snapstreaks, about a third of their hands go up. When I ask how many really like Snapstreaks, nearly all of the hands go down. It's the classic addict's narrative: They're doing something even though they don't really like it. They're trapped.

There's an even more serious issue: Drug dealers love Snapchat because posts disappear. The company's internal research found that half a million Snapchat users a day were exposed to drug-related content. The families of 64 young people who died from fentanyl overdoses sued the company for recommending that kids connect with drug dealers and allowing dealers to send them unsolicited lists of drugs for sale. When Michael Brewer was 11, he downloaded Snapchat and changed his birth year to circumvent the app's age-13 minimum. Two years later, he connected with a dealer on Snapchat and bought a Percocet he did not know was laced with fentanyl. Michael suffered a severe brain injury and is now blind and in a wheelchair. Out of the 64 plaintiffs, Michael is the star witness because only he and one other teen survived. The other 62 died.

- **Discord.** Discord is a site where groups of users can communicate. It started as a place for gamers having discussions but now hosts many types of groups. You need an account, but there are no algorithms. Sounds promising, but almost everyone on the site uses anonymous usernames, so it's very easy for adults to interact with children. Plus there are Discord groups that are dedicated to posting pornography and images of sexual abuse.

  A man on a Discord server persuaded a 14-year-old girl to send him a nude picture of herself, and then used it as blackmail to force her into filming degrading acts like drinking out of a toilet and even beheading her pet hamster. He and his accomplices then told her she needed to take video as she killed herself. Fortunately, she told her mother instead, and she survived. "People are not understanding the severity, the speed at which their children can become victimized," said Abbigail Beccaccio, chief of the FBI's Child Exploitation Operational Unit.

- **X/Twitter.** Most teens aren't interested in X as it tilts toward adults, so very few 15-and-unders will ask for an account here. It used to be a good news aggregator but isn't anymore as the algorithm now deprioritizes posts with links. Sexual content and ads for gambling do appear on the site, as do disturbing and violent videos; many users have noticed an increase in toxic content lately. It's become more video-based, but some still use it to communicate about ideas. It's best for kids to wait until 16 to access the site.

THE MAYBE LIST

- **WhatsApp.** This is a texting/messaging app that works between people who have each other's phone number. If you're OK with your kid sending texts, WhatsApp is probably fine. In one study of almost 500 teens, using WhatsApp helped teens feel closer to their friends and was not linked to unhappiness or low self-esteem. Still, be aware that group chats, especially if they get beyond about five people, can become performative in a way similar to Instagram. Like texting, WhatsApp can be distracting, can feature cyberbullying, and can replace conversations better had in real time. But it's not algorithmic and it's usually used for one-on-one communication.
- **YouTube.** YouTube doesn't require an account to watch videos, and it's often used by schools. That said, YouTube Shorts are very similar to TikTok, though with a somewhat less sticky algorithm. Most kids are going to see YouTube videos before they are 10. Don't allow the YouTube app on their phones and limit use of YouTube on their laptops. (See Rule 6 and Rule 9 for how to do this; the exact time limit may depend on whether your kid watches YouTube videos for homework. If they don't, 30 minutes a day is enough.) Make sure Autoplay is turned off on your kid's

account; otherwise, the next video will automatically start playing, which makes it much harder to stop watching. Especially for kids 12 and under, use YouTube Kids instead of the regular app or site, as its content is more appropriate for kids.

WAYS TO KEEP KIDS OFF

So how do you keep your kids off social media? In short, lock down their devices as much as possible. Specifically:

- **Do not give your kids a smartphone until they are at least 16.** When you do, put parental controls on it. The next three rules (Rules 4, 5, and 6) cover why and how to do this. Keeping kids off social media is one of the primary reasons for not giving your kid a smartphone until they are 16.

- **Avoid giving them their own tablet.** A tablet has all of the same abilities as a smartphone. Alexis Spence, who we met in the introduction, got her own tablet at 11 and at first mostly watched animal videos. But then she got Instagram, started spending so many hours on it she hid it from her parents behind a calculator app, and developed a severe eating disorder. If your kids use tablets on long trips, have them use a parent's tablet instead of giving a tablet of their own.

- **Block social media sites on their laptop (see the "no list," above).** By middle school, kids are often required to turn in homework online or watch videos for school, usually using a laptop. This is where things get tough, because they're probably using their laptop in their bedroom and you can't hover over them all the time. Although kids and teens usually access social media on phones, the apps are also accessible, though with fewer features, as websites on laptops. There's more on this in Rule 6 about parental controls and Rule 9 about laptops and gaming consoles.

- **Find other ways for kids to communicate.** Social media is far from the only way for kids to stay in touch with each other—they can text, call, or video chat with their friends on their own phone, or on yours if they don't have their own yet. Even better: They can go over to each other's home. If kids want to find information, they can do an internet search (preferably along with you if they are younger). All of these are better than algorithmic social media.

- **Be a good role model.** If you have social media, turn off notifications from the apps so you'll be more likely to use it only when you want to. Consider taking all social media apps off your phone and use them only on your computer or laptop—that will also make your choice more intentional and less likely to interfere with family time.

- **Discuss the pitfalls of social media with your kids.** This one is last, because talking isn't enough and the pull of the apps is strong. But especially as kids get older, discuss your reasoning with them. Share the charts in the introduction showing teen depression increasing and the links between social media and depression. Talk about how young people themselves describe the pressures of social media.

Also discuss how social media companies are making money off kids' time and attention. (Teens love the idea of adult conspiracies, and this actually is one!) According to one estimate, social media companies make $11 billion a year in advertising revenue from children and teens 17 and under. Two billion of that was from children 12 and under. A leaked email between two Meta employees put a monetary value on child users, noting that "the lifetime value of a 13 y/o teen is roughly $270 per teen."

Surely our children are worth more than that.

COMMON OBSTACLES AND PUSHBACKS

1. **"If I'm not on social media I will be left out."** Of course you don't want your kid to be left out. But you also don't want your kid to be exposed to the toxicity of social media. This is one of the main reasons parents give in to kids asking to have their own social media accounts, and one of the main reasons more regulation of social media would be amazing—then no one their age would have an account, and it wouldn't be an issue. Until then, it's up to parents to say no. (Mean moms are the best!)

   View this as a risk-benefit analysis. What is worse, being exposed to harmful content and risking depression and body image issues, or losing one mechanism for communicating with friends? Instead of using social media, kids can call or text their friends or, even better, get together in person (see Rule 8).

2. **"But I'll use it only to keep in touch with my friends—I promise."** Even if this is your kid's intention, they will soon run smack-dab into the algorithms designed to introduce them to new material so they will stay on the apps as long as possible. It's very difficult to only look at friends' content on social media and then get out—most adults can't do this, either.

3. **"If I don't have social media, I won't know what my friends are talking about."** Maybe, but maybe not. Social media pages are individualized—everyone's is different. Sure, some videos do go viral, but your kid can watch one or two on your phone or a friend's phone without having an account. And the memes? Kids talk about them so endlessly at school that your children will know them even without social media. And if they are interested in news or current events, there are many other places to find that information online (though you may have to tell them where to look). At one talk I gave at a high school, an 11th grader asked where he could get news if he didn't use social media. I told him to go to Google News—and it was clear he had no idea it existed.

4. **"But I really enjoy being on social media."** Not every kid will have negative experiences on social media. But it's impossible to tell who will and who won't at the beginning, and even then those experiences might change. Especially for kids 15 and under, the possible benefits are outweighed by the risks.

5. **"My sports team/club posts everything on social media."** This one is harder. You'll have to advocate for that to change

(hopefully with other parents). Ask the team or club to use group text or WhatsApp instead. Alternatively, you can follow the team on your own social media account, screenshot anything important, and text it to your kid.

6. **"I want to be able to communicate with other people like me."** If your kid has an interest or identity their classmates don't share, this is an understandable request. But kids don't necessarily need social media to do this—they have the rest of the internet.

   I've often heard the argument that LGBTQ+ teens in particular benefit from social media, but the evidence suggests otherwise. LGBTQ+ teens who are heavy users of social media are more likely to be depressed than light users, just like straight teens are. LGBTQ+ young adults are more likely to say the impact of social media on their emotional health was negative than non-LGBTQ+ young adults—probably because LGBTQ+ people experience more bullying online.

   Similarly, Black and Hispanic teens who are heavy users of social media are more likely to be depressed than light users. Plus, teens in these groups spend a staggering amount of time using social media: 35% of Black and 24% of Hispanic 8th and 10th grade girls spent seven or more hours a day on social media, compared to only 15% of White girls. That much time on social media crowds out time for sleep, schoolwork, and face-to-face time with friends and family. It's difficult to argue that social media is beneficial when it's filling the space of a full-time (unpaid!) job.

7. **"Social media is safe because the apps have special protections for kids."** Since age isn't verified, it's incredibly easy for kids to choose a different birth year and circumvent any restrictions for minors. Even if they set the right birthday, kids are still routinely exposed to inappropriate content and sexual solicitation. TikTok's own internal research concluded that their parental controls (Family Pairing) did not protect kids from sexual content. A 2025 report found that Instagram teen accounts—purportedly a safer version of the app—nevertheless regularly received content that was overtly sexual, related to body image issues or disordered eating, referenced alcohol or drugs, mentioned suicide or violence, or promoted toxic masculinity. App parental controls also do not eliminate the algorithms that draw kids in and keep them hooked, the reward structure of likes and followers, or the gamification of streaks. Better to keep kids off entirely.

8. **"But I want to take pictures and videos and share them with my friends."** There's a big difference between taking pictures and videos, which is a great creative outlet, and posting them on social media, which quickly becomes competitive and performative. Kids love taking goofy pictures of themselves and making silly videos. My photo app is filled with pictures of my kids scrunching up their faces into grotesque expressions after grabbing my phone or my husband's tablet. They also had fun making ridiculous videos—my all-time favorite is the fake movie trailer K made when she was 10 titled "The Scary Potty That Needed Cleaning," consisting primarily of closeups of the

aforementioned potty and her reeling back with her mouth open.

When kids get a social media account like Instagram, pictures and videos aren't for fun anymore. They're for popularity. That means hair and makeup done, perfect poses, and a carefully curated presence. It becomes work, not play.

So let your kids take pictures and videos, but tell them they're not for sharing. Make sure you have the conversation mentioned in Rule 1 about never, never taking nude pictures, and never sharing anything you wouldn't want spread around school.

If your kids don't have their own phone or tablet that takes pictures, buy them a stand-alone digital camera. E and J have great fun every year on our family vacation taking videos of each other hiding under the beds and then emerging to scare each other. They then watch the videos of each other screaming. That's not the type of content that gets likes on Instagram, but it's much more fun.

RULE 4: FIRST PHONES SHOULD BE BASIC PHONES

Logan Lane got her first smartphone in 6th grade, when she was 11. She soon downloaded social media apps and started to fall asleep with her phone next to her. "My immediate impulse was to use it all the time," she said at 17. By the time she got to high school, "I could not sleep. . . . I would stay up late most nights. I also developed this indent on my fingers, where I would be holding my phone because I was just so frequently scrolling with my hands in a particular position. . . . I was just blatantly unsatisfied with myself. I was constantly seeing something better that I could be. I developed this level of shame about who I wasn't."

As many parents and kids have found out the hard way, 10 or 11 is too young for a smartphone. It's not just the unfettered access to social media and the dark corners of the internet, which kids this age aren't even close to ready for. Smartphones also obstruct other experiences as kids are no longer interested in reading, playing with their siblings, going outside, or getting enough sleep. But these days, 10 or 11 is the average age for kids to get their first smartphone. Surely there has to be a better way.

There is, and it's three words (actually one word): Delay, delay, delay.

NO DEVICE OF THEIR OWN

My first piece of advice is simple: Delay giving your child *any* device of their own for as long as possible. That means no tablet, no phone, no smartwatch, and no gaming console that belongs just to them. I made this mistake early on. When our kids were young, in the early 2010s, we gave them each their own Kindle Fire (similar to an iPad). We set a limit of one hour a day for videos but allowed unlimited time for reading. I noticed the kids would watch their hour of video but would then put the tablet down like so much trash after that hour was up. They rarely if ever used it to read. I started to doubt the wisdom of their having their own devices. Then one day in 2016 I was analyzing some data for my book *iGen* (see Figure 4.1 on following page).

Every single activity on a screen was linked to more unhappiness, and every single activity that didn't involve a screen was instead linked to less unhappiness—and thus more happiness. Immediately after making this graph, I pushed my chair back from my desk, found the kids' Kindle Fires, and hid them in my dresser drawer.

I was surprised that it took several days for K to ask "Where's my Kindle Fire?" I told her we weren't going to use them anymore. That instantly gave my kids an hour a day more to do

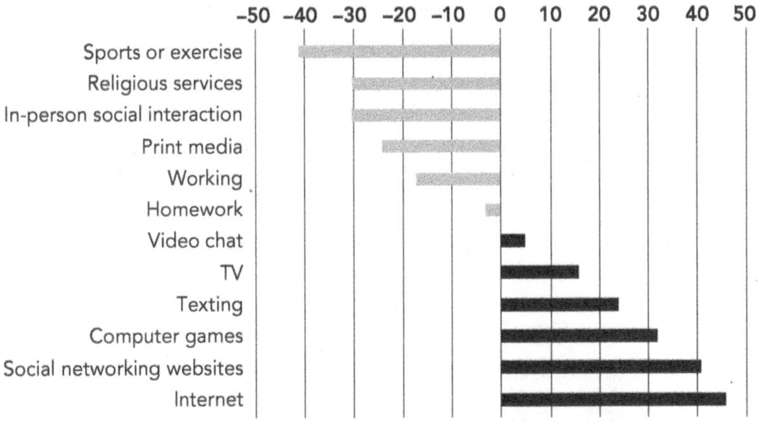

Figure 4.1: Increase or decrease in risk of unhappiness, screen and non-screen activities, U.S. 10th graders

Note: Black bars are screen device activities; gray bars are activities that do not involve a screen. Compares teens who spend more time on the activity versus less.

Source: Monitoring the Future survey, 2013–2015

other things. Often that was play outside. Sometimes it was fight with their sisters. (I figured they were building their relationship skills.) When they needed to use a tablet—like when their piano lessons moved to FaceTime during the pandemic—they borrowed my husband's iPad. It was much easier to make sure they weren't immersed in screens constantly when they had to ask to borrow an adult's device. (Once the school laptop appears in middle school it gets harder—more on this in Rule 9.)

You should also think twice, or three times, about giving your kid their own gaming console. If you do, don't put it in your kid's bedroom—it needs to go in a public space in the house and be shared by all family members. Then you'll be more aware of when your kid is gaming, and if their siblings also use it that might reduce the amount of time each spends gaming. Or they will play together, which is better than playing alone.

All of this goes double for kids having any type of mobile phone: Delay it for as long as possible. There is usually no compelling reason for elementary school kids to have any kind of phone. They walk home from school or take the bus? The chances of them needing to contact you are low. Generations of kids walked home from school by themselves without mobile phones. Your kids do activities and need to be picked up? Activities usually end at a set time. If you're not there right away, they can wait a few minutes. If it ends really early or is canceled, they can use a friend's phone or another parent's phone to reach you (have them memorize your phone number). They want to text their friends? They can borrow your phone to do that. Don't give them any type of phone or smartwatch until you have a very compelling reason. Think about it this way: When you don't give your kid a phone, you'll have one fight (over getting the phone) instead of thousands (every time they're on their phones when you'd rather they not be, which is usually Every. Single. Day. And usually multiple times a day).

Katherine Martinko's son was the only student in his high school without a smartphone. Other parents, she says, predictably ask her the same three questions. First, "Isn't he missing out?" Well yes, Martinko argues, he's missing spending all his leisure time on screens. Instead, he's biking with his friends, playing with his brothers, and learning how to cook. Smartphones are experience blockers. Once kids get one, a lot of other things stop happening. Put off that moment as long as possible.

Second, "What about safety?" Many kids with phones aren't paying attention to what's around them, so they may even be less safe if they have a phone. Many pedestrian-car accidents happen when the pedestrian, including kids, are looking at their phones. And then there's the unregulated online world, which is also not safe for kids.

Third, "Aren't you ruining his future professional opportunities?" No, Martinko says, these technologies are designed to be intuitive—plus they are always changing, so who knows what the new app will be when he's ready to start his career? She's right: Social media companies purposefully make their apps as easy to use as possible. Kids can learn how to use the apps when they are ready, and it won't take them long.

TYPES OF PHONES—AND WHAT TO CALL THEM

At some point, you're going to consider getting your kid a phone. Maybe the closest bus stop is far away and the bus isn't always on time. Maybe your kid is going to be flying on a plane without you. Maybe you're tired of their borrowing your phone to text their friends. Maybe they're going into high school and it seems like the right time. What type of phone should you get them?

Let's start by getting our terms straight. I'm going to use *smartphone* to mean an internet-enabled phone—iPhones and Android phones that have a web browser, email, and unfettered access to social media and other apps. Smartphones are only one type of mobile phone. There are three other major types:

1. **Flip phones.** These are the old-school phones you might remember from the 2000s. They can make calls and send texts and maybe play a few simple games, and that's it. I'm

not talking about a foldable Samsung Galaxy. A flip phone has no internet access.

2. **Smartwatches.** Most smartwatches allow the user to call, text, play games, and listen to music. I don't mean an activity watch that counts steps. A good test: If it can send texts, it's a smartwatch.

3. **Basic phones.** These are phones that can call and text but do not have internet access or social media apps. They may have other features depending on the brand. These phones go by a variety of names, but let's call them *basic phones*. If you call it a "kids phone," teens won't want to use it because it's for kids. Even younger kids over age nine may not want to use it if they think it's for "little kids." "Kids phone" also isn't accurate as there are some versions of basic phones used by adults. An alternative term is *minimal phone*. Consider using that term instead if your kid says "that's so basic" a lot and doesn't mean anything good by it.

As you'll learn in Rule 5, it's best to give a kid their first smartphone only when they get their driver's license (or are at least 16 and getting around independently). One choice is to not give your kid any type of phone until 16. Another option is to give them a flip phone, smartwatch, or basic phone—then they can call, text, and do a few other things on their phones, but there's no internet and no social media. In one study, adults who gave up internet access on their phone for a month ended up happier and with longer attention spans.

And that doesn't even consider the long-term effects of kids having smartphones when their brains are still developing.

CHOOSING THE RIGHT FIRST PHONE

So what type of non-smartphone should you give your kid? Let's consider each type.

Flip phones

If your kid travels by themself and they only need a phone for calling and simple texting, flip phones are a good option. Brands include Cricket Wireless, Nokia, Tracfone, and Jitterbug. Flip phones can make calls nearly everywhere a smartphone can make calls.

One advantage of a flip phone is how little it can do. There's no internet, no social media, and only a limited number of games. Since there's no keyboard, texting involves pressing the number keys multiple times for one letter (if you had a cellphone in the 2000s, you probably remember this). Texts are going to be short. That means your kid won't be constantly texting their friends, because it takes too long. As they get older, this can turn into a disadvantage if their friends communicate via text and it's difficult for them to reply.

Flip phones also stand out. Unlike basic phones, they don't look like a smartphone, so other kids will notice it's not the same. When K was in 9th grade and had a flip phone, one of her peers offered to buy her a "real phone." Fortunately, K thought that was funny; not every kid would. Some people call flip phones "burner phones" or even "drug dealer phones."

Smartwatches

Many parents get their kids a smartwatch as a first mobile device. Watches designed for kids (such as a Gabb, Bark, Troomi, or Gizmo watch) are stand-alone devices, while Apple Watches need to be connected to a smartphone (which can be a parent's phone if you set up the watch with Apple's Family Sharing).

Some watches have speech-to-text, making it easier for kids to text. Parents can remotely enable quiet times when kids need to focus so they don't get calls or texts. Some watches also allow kids to take photos and videos. Parents like these devices since they can contact their kids, but kids can't do too much on the watch. They can still be very distracting, though. Before you buy one, make sure you know exactly what features kids can access and what they can't. For example, on Apple Watches kids might be able to buy things using Apple Pay and access YouTube via an app called WatchTube. Also ensure they can't access social media on it. If you consider a smartwatch, make sure you can easily set up a focus or quiet mode, especially after bedtime and during school hours. Elementary school teachers—even those who teach 2nd or 3rd grade—increasingly say that kids are texting, playing games, and even checking social media on their smartwatches during the school day. Remember, put off giving kids any device of their own as long as possible. That includes smartwatches.

BASIC PHONES

Basic phones are safer for kids right out of the box, with built-in parental controls that are easier to use and harder to hack than those on smartphones. With no internet or social media, it's a lot less likely unknown adults will be able to randomly contact your kid, and kids are not going to stumble across pornography. Basic phones are usually Android phones with a modified operating system, so they look like a regular smartphone.

Even these pared-down phones can be distracting, so wait as long as possible before getting your kid one. We gave our youngest, J, a basic phone when she started 6th grade, mostly because her middle school bus stop was a mile away. It worked out OK, but she still had it in her hand way too often. If I had to do it over again, I'd have gotten her a flip phone instead and would have put off even the basic phone until 8th or 9th grade. Later, I tried to correct somewhat by putting time limits on the apps that were the most distracting, which helped.

But if your kid wants a phone that looks like everyone else's that they can use to easily text their friends, basic phones are the way to go. They're the training wheels of phones.

Each brand of basic phone is a little different, and since the technology keeps changing you'll want to do your own research online to get the most up-to-date information. Here's a brief overview of the different types of basic phones, from those with the fewest capabilities to the most:

- **Gabb Phone 4:** This is the most basic of the basic phones, with calling, texting (including text-to-speech), clean music streaming, and a camera, but no capability for adding additional third-party apps. "You can't do anything on it," E said about her Gabb phone. "That," I replied, "is the point." If this is what you want, make sure you're buying the Gabb Phone 4 and not the Pro, which allows more apps.

- **Pinwheel, Troomi, Gabb Phone 4 Pro, Bark.** These are basic phones that have access to an app store to add additional features. They come with an online parent portal where you can set a schedule (like having the phone shut off at bedtime) and approve new contacts. Some allow you to see the texts your child has received and sent.

  The parent portal also lets you see the apps available for the phone. You can then install those you want or approve (or reject) those your kids ask for. These phones don't allow certain apps at all (mostly dating, pornography, and alcohol-related apps, as well as those that allow contact with unknown adults). That's a relief, but there are still tough decisions about what to allow versus not (more on this in a sec). The trade-off for more flexibility is more complexity in managing the phone.

  Still, I'd much rather have this challenge than giving a 12-year-old a smartphone with internet and social media access. Basic phones' ability to remotely control bedtime, approve or disapprove app installs, and set time limits for apps after you've given the kid the phone is also essential. At ages 13 and 15, my younger two children both have basic phones like these.

- **The Light Phone.** This is a grown-up basic phone. Unlike other basic phones, it's not necessarily meant for kids, and it's not an Android phone—it's a unique device. It has a paper-like screen like a Kindle, so it's not as colorfully tempting as a smartphone. It has a maps app, calling, and texting, but does not have internet access, social media, or email. The newest version has a camera. All of the features are optional, so you can choose which features your kid has. Many adults who want a pared-down phone, sometimes just for certain situations, use Light Phones. That also means it doesn't come with a parent portal like the phones designed for kids.

WHICH APPS DO YOU ALLOW?

The biggest challenge with basic phones (with the exception of the more limited Gabb Phone 4) is deciding which apps to allow. The parent portals for these products give more information and sometimes even a rating for each app, but it's often hard to judge what's appropriate and what's not without using the app yourself.

The Pinwheel portal, for example, rates apps as "Pinwheel Approved," "Slightly Out of Bounds," "Violates Guidelines," and "Untested by Pinwheel." The middle two categories have some features outside Pinwheel's guidelines. If you're wondering why the apps that violate guidelines are there at all, it's often because they are required by schools or clubs (for example, Google Drive, Canvas).

If you click on the rating under the app it will usually note the not-kid-safe issues the company found, like "contacts: child managed," "anonymous communication allowed," "consumption & addictive design," and "web access possible" (some apps have a backdoor into the web if, as Pinwheel puts it, "your child looks hard enough"). You'll have to judge how much these things matter to you, especially since even apps in the same category can vary a lot. For example, when E was going to fly on Delta by herself, I installed the Delta app even though it's categorized under "Violates Guidelines" (mostly due to potential loopholes into the web). In contrast, the Alaska Airlines app is Pinwheel Approved. Very random.

It's especially difficult to judge which games to allow. I've never played phone games, and even if I had, the popular games seem to change every month. I find it tough to tell which games are appropriate, not addictive, etc. Is Subway Surfers appropriate? (Given that the kid in the logo has a spray-paint can, I'm guessing not, but E really wants it.) Chess for Kids sounds innocuous, but it violates Pinwheel guidelines because it uses addictive design techniques. I ended up blocking Subway Surfers and leaving Chess for Kids.

Even kid-appropriate apps can be a problem. E and J use Duolingo so they can learn Spanish, but I'm not a fan of the whole "But, Mom, I need my phone on vacation so I don't break my Duolingo streak!" (A streak is the number of days in a row they have used the app.) I'm also ambivalent to negative on the "art" apps, like the one J uses to do paint by numbers. After all, there's no physical painting to hang on the wall at the end, so what's the point? But she says she has nothing else to do on the bus, so I allowed it but put a time limit on it.

One other issue to be aware of: All of these apps display ads, and the ads—even on a so-called "kids phone"—are not filtered. Your kid might be playing "Find the Cat" and be served ads for AI girlfriends. They won't be able to download the AI girlfriend app, thank goodness, but you may find yourself explaining what an AI girlfriend is to a 10-year-old. If that's a nonstarter, you may have to say no to any app with ads, which includes Duolingo and all games.

Then there's Spotify, which my kids use to listen to music. Sounds good, except Spotify has a backdoor to YouTube. J tells me that it only links to certain podcasts on YouTube, but which ones? And how do I know she can't play other YouTube videos on it? Plus, the app is rated 17+ because of the type of data it collects from users, and it has unfiltered content. But when we tried other music apps, like Amazon Music, we couldn't get them to work on her phone. I'm hoping in the future more apps will work seamlessly on basic phones.

If you do allow games and music, block them during school hours if your kids' school still allows phones during the school day. That way you'll know your kids are paying attention in class instead of playing *Block Blast*. And if they say they want to play games during lunch, tell them they should be talking to their friends then.

COMMON OBSTACLES AND PUSHBACKS

1. **"But they need a phone to be safe."** This argument may come from spouses, grandparents, or fellow parents. Ironically, none of these people had a phone when they were a kid, yet they now consider a phone essential for safety. And how, exactly, does having a phone keep kids safe? It's not going to prevent them from getting injured while walking—in fact they're going to be more likely to get hit by a car if they are distracted by their phone. Having a phone is very unlikely to prevent your kid being the victim of a crime—again, they might be more distracted. (There's more on safety in Rule 8.) Overall, the likelihood that a kid will end up in an unsafe situation because they *have*

a phone is much higher than the likelihood that they will end up in an unsafe situation because they *don't* have a phone.

2. **"But I'm the only one who doesn't have a smartphone."** One mom told me her 12-year-old son made a list of 25 reasons he wanted a phone and then lengthened it to 50. Most of the reasons, she told me, were some version of "because all of my friends have one." If that sounds like your kid, tell them different families have different rules, and it's usually not a good idea to do something just because everyone else is doing it. And hold firm.

   Another solution is to team up with other parents who also don't want to give their children smartphones until later. One group that's doing that is called Wait Until 8th. It's a grassroots organization founded by an Austin, Texas, mom that allows parents to sign a pledge saying they won't give their kids smartphones until, at the earliest, the end of 8th grade. The group also encourages parents to set limits on smartphones after kids get them, including blocking app downloads and disabling the internet browser. In Australia, groups like Wait Mate and the Heads Up Alliance use similar pledges. These groups organize parents at the same school so their kid won't be the "only one" in their grade without a smartphone. Dany and Claudia Elachi, who we met in the introduction, founded the Heads Up Alliance after their experience with their oldest daughter. Even if you don't join an organization like this, talk to your kids' friends' parents about not giving them smartphones until later.

3. **"But I'm/they're a good kid."** Sometimes you'll hear this from your kid. Sometimes you'll hear it from your spouse. This is the idea that kids who aren't troublemakers won't try to open a social media account without permission, watch YouTube when they are supposed to be doing their homework, or hide a device in their bed. All three of my kids are so-called "good kids," and all three of them did one or more of these things anyway. The pull of the apps is very strong even for kids who are otherwise rule-followers. Plus, kids often stumble across pornography and other inappropriate material accidentally, so it's not just a matter of what they seek out or do voluntarily. This is not a good reason to give them a phone.

4. **"Instead of basic phones, why not give kids smartphones and have them sign a cellphone contract?"** Cellphone contracts—a list of phone rules and the consequences for breaking them—are a great idea. They're just not enough. Most cellphone contracts have rules such as "I will never join social media apps without permission," or "I will never open or view pages that are not allowed." Those are good rules, but also very tempting for kids to break. And how will parents even know if their kid has social media apps on their phone or visited an inappropriate site? Better to instead give kids a basic phone that doesn't have these options at all. That said, you should absolutely consider printing out a cellphone contract and going over it with your kid before they get their first basic phone. Many contracts have useful rules like "If asked to stop using my phone, I will happily do so," and "I will give my parents

access to my phone whenever." It makes sense to clearly spell out expectations for kids having phones, even basic phones. The combination of a contract and a basic phone is much more powerful than the contract alone. You can also make a new contract once they get a smartphone.

5. **"It's embarrassing to have a phone made for kids."** Who's going to know? Basic phones designed for kids, like Gabb and Troomi, look like a regular Android phone. E once told me she was embarrassed when a friend asked her "What kind of phone is that?" I told her she could honestly answer "It's an Android phone." There's also no need to disclose that the phone doesn't allow social media or internet. If your friends ask if you have a certain app and you don't, I told E, just say your parents don't allow it. All kids understand that parents are lame. :)

RULE 5: GIVE THE FIRST SMARTPHONE WITH THE DRIVER'S LICENSE

When K was 11, she flew cross-country by herself to stay with a friend for a week. We bought her a cheap flip phone mostly so she could contact her friend's dad at the airport. She also used it for another purpose: Every morning, she would send me a five-letter, all-caps text: "ALIVE."

When she returned from the trip, she handed the phone back to me. That happened every summer, so during the school year the phone sat in a drawer gathering dust. By 9th grade, though, K started using the flip phone more regularly. She didn't really mind standing out—she said being "the kid with the flip phone" became part of her identity. On one family trip, the guy standing behind her at the airport burger place remarked loudly, "Bro's so broke he's gotta use a flip phone." Her short haircut meant she was used to being mistaken for a boy, but being assumed to be penniless based on her phone was a new one.

Then, three weeks after her 16th birthday, she got her driver's license. A few months later, she got lost on the way to a swim meet while using printed directions and had to call us for help.

That's when we decided to get her a smartphone. And the more I thought about it, the more this made sense as a general rule: Kids get their first internet-enabled phone when they get their driver's license.

THE WHY BEHIND THE RULE

There are three solid reasons for linking the first smartphone to a driver's license:

1. **Before a teen starts driving, they don't really need a smartphone.** No-internet phones work just fine, especially since your middle-school- or high-school-age kid probably has a laptop (either their own or the school's) to access the internet when they need it. But once teens start driving, having the maps app and internet access can be very useful. At 16, they are also more likely to start doing things like going to concerts or going shopping without a parent along, and an internet-enabled phone is useful in those situations. If your kid walks or takes public transportation to school or elsewhere, the rule can easily be modified: When they are at least 16 and can get places on their own, they can get a smartphone.

2. **At 16, kids are starting to develop better decision-making.** That's why we trust 16-year-olds to drive, but not 14-year-olds. Plus, since 16 is the minimum age kids should get social media (Rule 3), no smartphone until 16 helps ensure 15-and-unders haven't downloaded a social media app

without your knowledge. If they don't have a smartphone, there is one less device you have to worry about—and the smartphone is the most worrisome as it's the smallest and most portable device.

3. **A driver's license means more opportunities for seeing friends in person.** Many younger teens spend a lot of time on their phones partially because they don't have the freedom to get together with their friends in person (more on this in Rule 8). Under this rule, the smartphone comes when they have the option of getting in the car and going to their friends' houses. And if you have a teen who is reluctant to get their license, the promise of a smartphone might help motivate them to take this step toward independence.

16 IS BETTER THAN 14

Why not 14 or the beginning of high school as the age to get a smartphone, as some other books and experts have suggested? The beginning of high school is already a difficult time. Academic expectations ramp up, friendships shift, and kids are still trying to figure out who they are and where they fit in. By 16, they have settled into high school and are more mature. And again, they don't really *need* an internet-enabled phone at 14. Why not put it off as long as possible?

Even parents who delay giving their kids smartphones until high school often wish they'd delayed even longer. One mother who gave her 15-year-old a smartphone said, "I wish I hadn't. If I could go back and do it over, I'd delay even longer. It created more problems than it was worth." Another said her son immediately had trouble putting the phone down. "He can't resist it," she said. "It has changed so much."

Some families use a variant on this rule that also puts off the smartphone until 16 or later: You can have a smartphone when you can buy it yourself. That connects the smartphone to the mature responsibility of making and saving money. It also has the advantage of kids having more respect for how much the phone costs—they'll be less likely to break it or lose it if they know they'll have to earn the money to replace it.

Another argument for delaying the smartphone is the research on mental health. The later a young person got their first smartphone, the better their mental health in young adulthood (see Figure 5.1 on the following page). The difference was especially large for girls. Overall, it suggests that the rule for smartphones is the later the better. You could even argue for waiting until 18 given this graph.

"BUT EVERYONE ELSE HAS ONE"

"Everyone else has one" is not a compelling reason to get a kid a smartphone. When I was a kid, parents didn't usually cave in when a kid said this. Yet today, when parents hear that everyone else has a phone, that's taken as a valid argument. If your kid is the last one in their class to get a smartphone, that means you won. Especially if they have a basic phone and can text their friends, "but everyone else has one" is not the mic drop it's made out to be. So what?

Plus, once your kids get to early adulthood, the chances are good they will thank you. When I talk to college students about phones and social media, those who had parents who put restrictions on them say they are grateful.

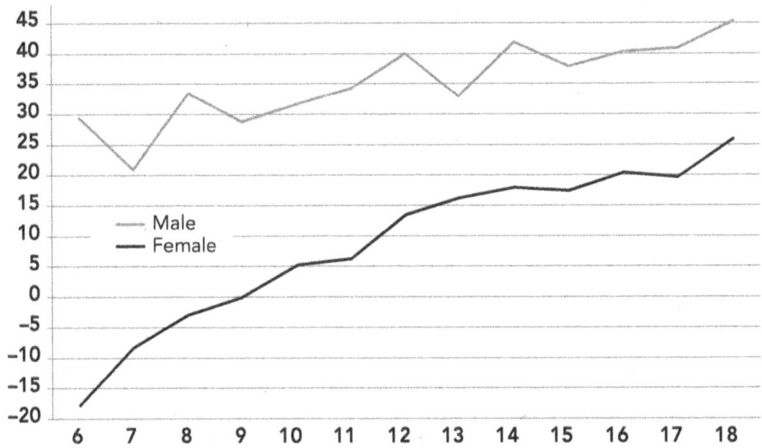

Figure 5.1: Mental health by age of first smartphone ownership

Source: Sapien Labs study of 27,969 18- to 24-year-olds around the world, 2023

All of that said, it's true kids hate being the only one who doesn't have a phone. As noted in Rule 4, many parents are joining groups like Wait Until 8th to pledge to not give their kids smartphones until later so their kids aren't the only ones in their grade without a smartphone. This can also be done informally if you talk to the parents of your kids' friends. But it's nice to have it coordinated, especially if it feels awkward to bring it up in casual conversation.

CHOOSING THE RIGHT SMARTPHONE AND SETTING IT UP

Compared to buying a basic phone, buying a regular smartphone is easy. There are lots of options, with iPhones and Android phones the most popular. Your choice of a smartphone brand will depend on your budget, the features you want most, and what the rest of the family uses.

But what if your 16-year-old with a new driver's license is, in your opinion or theirs, not quite ready for a smartphone? Or you'd really like to wait until they're 18 or out of your house to have the internet and social media in their pocket? One option is the Light Phone, covered in the last chapter. It has a maps app with driving directions, so it's more practical for a new driver than the other types of basic phones.

Even with a 16-year-old, you don't want to just hand your kid a smartphone. The process should be gradual. For example, getting a driver's license involves obtaining a learner's permit and then a license with restrictions. Similarly, getting your first smartphone should resemble wading into the water, not jumping into the deep end.

Before you give your kid a phone, set it up so their entry into this experience is slow instead of abrupt. This is your chance to curate the initial experience your kid will have with their phone. Do it now, not later: Wresting the phone out of your kid's grasp or having to ask for their passcode after you've given them the phone will be a lot harder. There are two things to do right away:

1. **Set up parental controls** (see Rules 6 and 9 for more details).

2. **Turn off notifications for everything except for calls and texts.** Kids 11 to 17 get an average of 237 notifications a *day*. Notifications are one of the main reasons kids (and adults) can't put down their phones. Your kid doesn't need social media, email, and news notifications rolling in all of the time—they can go to these apps a few times a day instead

of getting drawn back in. They'll still get lots of notifications from texts and that will be distracting enough—but at least those are usually from friends. Talk to your kid about why it's better to keep most notifications off.

Once you've done these things, you can give your newly minted driver their first smartphone. They will be pretty fascinated by it for a while, and you'll have to make your expectations clear about when and where they can use it (see Rules 2 and 7). The chances are good they'll be pulling it out of their pocket constantly. It takes some getting used to. One thing I can virtually guarantee: You will not be sorry you waited.

COMMON OBSTACLES AND PUSHBACKS

1. **"I need a smartphone so I can take pictures of my homework to turn it in."** E told me this at the beginning of her 9th grade year, when she had a basic phone without email or internet. I told her to take a picture using her laptop. I knew this would work as that's what K did during 9th grade and most of 10th grade. I told E she could also use her digital camera and then plug in the SD card to her laptop.

2. **"But I'm ready to get a phone even though I'm not 16."** Or, as phrased by an adult, "Aren't kids different? Maybe some are ready for a phone earlier." Maybe, but it's easier to have a straightforward rule, and we have to draw the line somewhere. Some kids might be ready to drive at 15, and some not until 18, but 16 is the minimum age for driving in most U.S. states. We chose an age and stuck with it. We should do the same for phones.

3. **"I can't pair my phone with my laptop."** That one is easy—good! I don't want you getting text notifications fed to your laptop when you are doing your homework. This is actually a more common complaint from parents—I sometimes wish E and J had iPhones so I could text them from my computer, which is much easier for a Gen Xer like me. On the other hand, having to peck out texts is a good reminder that I should probably call them instead.

4. **"My phone can't do X or Y."** It's true that basic phones have some limitations. We were never able to find a music app other than Spotify that worked on our kids' basic phones. The kids not having internet access on their phones was a pain sometimes. But these are minor inconveniences that are worth it for them to be more protected online until they are 16.

5. **"You'll regret not giving your kid a smartphone earlier,"** said no one ever. I've never heard a parent say this. Instead, everyone says they regretted not waiting longer to give their kid a phone. Even though K didn't get a smartphone until she was almost sixteen and a half, I wish we had waited even longer. I'm writing this on the day of her 18th birthday, six weeks before she graduates from high school. That makes me reflect on how short childhood is, and how precious those years with our children are. I am nothing but grateful that the distraction of the smartphone was in her pocket for less of that time instead of more.

RULE 6:
USE PARENTAL CONTROLS

A few years ago, I visited a friend who had three teenage boys. We were discussing what kids do on their phones when I mentioned how old boys usually are when they first see pornography online (which is, depressingly, age 10 or 11). "I don't think my boys are watching porn—we watch all kinds of shows like *Game of Thrones* that are pretty close to porn anyway," she said. She called in her oldest son, who was 15 at the time. "Do you watch porn on your phone?" she asked. He looked sheepish and nodded, a blush moving up his face.

It's not just porn or inappropriate content. Stories abound of teens getting addicted to their phones, opening social media accounts without their parents' knowledge, and endlessly watching videos when they're supposed to be doing homework or sleeping.

This doesn't have to happen.

When a teen gets their first smartphone, it's very tempting to just hand the phone over. Resist that urge. They still need a few guardrails, and one way to put those guardrails in place is to use parental controls.

Even if your kid doesn't have a smartphone yet, you'll still want to read this chapter. Most kids 11 and up have their own laptop to do homework, and you'll want to put parental controls on it. (Assuming you can; school-provided laptops don't allow parental controls. More on this in Rule 9.) You will also want to install parental controls if your kid has their own tablet.

Studies have found that when parents monitor device use, kids are much less likely to be heavy users and are less likely to suffer from depression, dissatisfaction with life, or insecurity about their appearance. Not only will your kids be safer, but you'll feel better: A set of studies found that parents who used parental control software were less stressed and happier.

There are five parental controls that are particularly important:

1. **No downloading apps without permission.** This is most useful for phones: If your kid wants to download an app, a parent has to enter their passcode. This is important because then if your 16-year-old wants to use social media, you can have a conversation about it first rather than them making a unilateral decision in the moment. And maybe you're OK with your 16-year-old having social media on their laptop, but not on their phone, where it has more features and is accessible all the time. They'll spend less time on YouTube if it's only on their laptop and not on their phone.

   It's not just social media. There are all kinds of apps you probably don't want your teen using—dating apps, gambling apps, AI girlfriends and boyfriends, pornography apps, adult games, apps that allow you to chat with random strangers. The parent portal for the Pinwheel phone—one of the basic phones I mentioned in Rule 4—has a long list of apps it always bans. They include "3way: Threesome Hookup Dating," "777 slots—Vegas Casino Slot!" "Adult Sexy Coloring Games," "AI Girlfriend—Mate Simulator," "Anonymous Chat (Random Chat)," "App Hider," "Bang City—No Strings Dating," and "BlackJack 21 Pro." And those are just a few highlights. Eye opening, to say the least.

If you don't block app downloads on your teen's phone, there's nothing stopping them from downloading apps like these. They can even use an app hider so you never know they have "Bang City" on their phone. That's why this parental control is necessary even for older teens.

Not allowing app downloads also blocks a common end-run around time limits. Kids sometimes uninstall an app and then reinstall it, which strips away all parental controls. If they can't download apps, though, then they can't do this.

On an iPhone, you can block app downloads under Screen Time, Content & Privacy Restrictions, and iTunes & App Store Purchases. Turn everything to Don't Allow. We kept this control on K's phone until a few weeks after she turned 18.

2. **Time limits.** Your 16-year-old really wants to see what the big deal is with Instagram, Snapchat, or TikTok? If you think they're ready, OK: But set a daily time limit. Social media algorithms are sticky, so it's common to intend to spend a few minutes on the app and then look up to find 30 minutes or more has passed. Set a time limit so the app shuts down after the time limit is up. I'd suggest no

more than an hour a day total for all social media (including video apps like TikTok). So if they have Instagram and TikTok, they get 30 minutes on each. Even in 10th grade, when most students are 16, more time on social media is still linked to more depression (see Figure 6.1). The link weakens somewhat as kids get older, but it doesn't go away.

The same goes for games on phones—no more than an hour a day total. The problem is they might have 10 games. If so, a time limit of 30 minutes per day each adds up to five hours—way too much. Have your kid choose three games and rank them. They can get 30 minutes a day

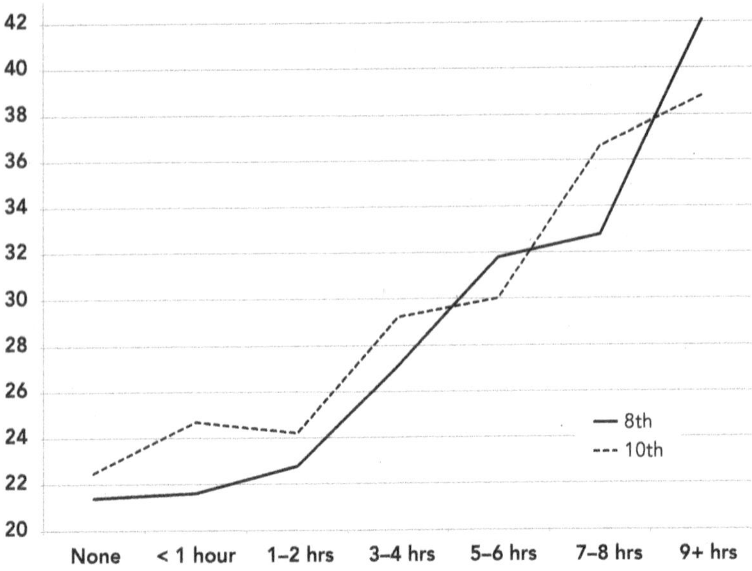

Figure 6.1: Hours per day of social media use and depression, U.S. 8th and 10th graders

Source: Monitoring the Future survey, 2018–2023

Note: Controlled for sex, race, mother's education level, and frequency of in-person social interaction. Depressive symptoms are measured by a six-item scale, and teens are considered depressed if their average score is a 3 or above on a 5-point scale.

on their favorite and 15 minutes on the other two, or 20 minutes on each.

3. **It's not very interesting after bedtime.** Set the controls so the device has limited capabilities when your child is supposed to be sleeping—for example, 10 p.m. to 7 a.m. for a 16-year-old who needs nine hours of sleep and needs to be up by seven on school days. It's supposed to be out of their room anyway (see Rule 2), but then if mistakes are made they won't be scrolling through Instagram at 2 a.m. Even better, have the phone go into sleep mode 30 to 60 minutes before bedtime (say, 9:30 p.m.) so they have some non-screen-time before bed (see Rule 7).

   You can make some apps (like calling and Maps) always available but block others. That way your kid with a driver's license can still find their way home or call for help after bedtime—they just can't watch TikTok or play games at 3 a.m. There are circumstances when a teen might need access to a phone after bedtime, but there's no reason they'd need access to social media in the middle of the night. Shut down access to these apps during sleep time.

4. **It's not very interesting during school hours.** Set up the phone so only a limited number of apps (say, calling) are available during school hours. Block social media and games and consider blocking texting. Until more schools ban phones during the whole school day (see Rule 10), kids are distracted by phones in class and playing games at lunch when they should be talking with their friends, with negative impacts on their academic performance and social skills.

5. **Block inappropriate websites and social media.** Which websites should you block? That's going to differ based on your family, your kids, and which sites are currently active. One clear candidate is Pornhub. To access Pornhub, all you have to do is go to the site and click on an orange box that says "I am 18 or older—Enter" and you are immediately taken to a page with explicit videos that are already rolling. Age isn't verified. (Pornhub's excuse? "We firmly believe that parents are best placed to police their children's activity using the plethora of tools already available in modern operating systems and devices.") So, without parental controls, any kid with an electronic device can see explicit pornography anytime they want. This is why parental controls are essential.

   Blocking all inappropriate websites may take some research. Pornhub isn't the only porn site, of course, so you'll have to find a list (Google "sites to block from kids"). Also block dating sites, chat rooms where kids can meet unknown adults, gambling sites, online forums with extreme content (like 4chan), and sites with violent content (like LiveLeak.com). If your kid has a laptop and is 15 or under, you'll want to block social media sites as well. Third-party software makes blocking websites much easier—I'll cover that in a minute.

SEEING WHAT KIDS ARE DOING: YES OR NO?

Notice that none of the five controls above involve seeing what your kids are texting or what they are viewing online. That's partially because I'm assuming you've waited to give your kid a smartphone until they are 16, when they will want (and hopefully will have earned) more privacy. When teens complain about parents monitoring their devices, lack of privacy is almost always their primary issue. They feel their parents shouldn't be seeing what they are texting their friends. I get that—I wouldn't have wanted my parents listening in on my phone conversations when I was a teen.

But if your kid is struggling with bullying or mental health issues, you might want to see what they're doing on their devices. This is more of a judgment call and an individual family decision rather than a straightforward rule like the rest in this book. Most third-party parental control software will let you see what your kids are doing on their phones.

SETTING UP PARENTAL CONTROLS

Ideally, you'll want to set up parental controls before giving your child the device. If your kid already has a device, though, you can still put parental controls on it. Tell your child that they need to share their passcode with you. Emphasize that you don't particularly want to read their text messages—you just want to put controls on the device so it's safer for them. Tell them you want to make sure they don't see things they can't unsee (I've used this language with my kids many times). If they still refuse, they lose the privilege of using the device and you take it until they share the passcode.

You have two choices for parental controls on a device: those built into the operating system and third-party software.

- **Operating system controls.** The upside of operating system controls is they are free and integrated with the device.

The downside is they can be difficult to use and are not as comprehensive as many parents would like.

You can find instructions about how to set up parental controls for different devices online. For an iPhone, for example, go to the Settings App and then Screen Time. You'll need to choose a numerical passcode (make sure it's not something your kids will guess). In Downtime, you can toggle on Scheduled and set the time that the device shuts off most apps at bedtime. In Always Allowed, you can set which apps can be accessed even during Downtime (for example, calling and maps). In App Limits, you can set a time limit on certain categories of apps or certain apps. Social media, for example, will be under Social. Messages (texting) and FaceTime are also in that category.

If you want to be able to change the Screen Time settings on an iPhone remotely, you have to set up Apple Family Sharing. That means everyone, including the kids, needs an Apple Account. For kids 13 and older, for you to change settings they have to enter their Apple Account password on your phone or respond to a text (in other words, this only works if you get buy-in from your kids—which isn't always practical). Android phones have a similar system under Google Family Link. If you don't use Family Sharing or Link, you'll have to go into your kid's phone or laptop to change the parental control settings. That means physically getting the device and getting their password or passcode out of them Every. Single. Time. you need to make a change.

In my experience, operating system parental controls are difficult to set up and limited in their capabilities. It's not easy to figure out where to find each of the controls in the settings, some of the interfaces are confusing, and website blocking capability is very limited. Turns out I'm not the only one. When Louisiana state representative Kim Carver tried to pass a law requiring Apple to enforce age restrictions on apps, the company's lobbyists told him that Apple devices already included parental control tools. When Carver later tried to set up parental controls on his 14-year-old's new iPhone, though, he found the company had oversold their system. "I quickly realized Apple's parental controls aren't the panacea they're promised to be," he said, echoing the experience of many parents.

- **Third-party software.** The downside of third-party parental control software is that these programs cost money (though usually not too much—most are less than $70 a year, and that can cover multiple kids and multiple devices). The upside is they are much easier to use than operating system controls and can do much more. For example, when you use the operating system controls, how do you know that you've blocked all of the porn and dating sites? That's almost impossible to do since there are so many and they keep changing. But third-party software can filter out whole categories of websites, including porn, alcohol, and gambling. Examples of third-party parental control software products are Aura, Bark, Canopy, Net Nanny, OurPact, and Qustodio.

  Best of all, these programs allow you to control your kid's device remotely. Your kid has been using their phone in the middle of the night when they're not supposed to? You can disable the phone during overnight hours from your own phone or computer. Your kid is spending way too much time on their laptop? You can set a time limit without having to physically access their device. I have reluctantly concluded that third-party software is the only practical way to protect kids' and teens' devices. Fortunately, you can do that while spending less per year than you do for a streaming service. That's still not equitable or fair, but that's where we are.

Before buying third-party parental control software, make sure that the software will work on your kid's device. All of these programs work on Androids and iPhones, but when I was considering buying E and J their own Mac laptops, it was difficult to determine which programs would work on a Mac computer. You'll want to look for a list of compatible operating systems. Sometimes that's under Help or Support. Other times I had to leave the website, go to Google, and type in "Mac laptop" and the name of the software. You can do the same with the device your kid has. Be aware that sometimes that will take you to a page for setting up the parent dashboard on your laptop, not for installing the software on a kid's laptop. (All of this should be easier!) There's much more on third-party software—including my own experience installing it—in Rule 9.

WHO SHOULD SET UP THE PARENTAL CONTROLS? THE DILEMMA

You'll also have to decide which parent will set up the parental controls. In many families, the parent who wants stricter rules for kids' tech use is also the parent who is less tech-savvy. That might not be a coincidence. If that's your situation and you are the less tech-savvy parent, you have a few choices:

1. **Take the plunge and learn how to set up the controls yourself.** Signing up for third-party software will probably be the easiest route as those programs are more user-friendly than the operating system controls.

2. **Sit down together with your partner to set up your children's devices and parental controls.** Then you can see exactly what your more tech-oriented partner is doing. But if they are in charge of maintaining the controls (say, approving apps for your kid to download), you'll have to make sure to have frequent check-ins.

3. **Have the more lenient but more tech-savvy parent set up the parental controls on their own and then show you what they've done.** Then you can make sure the controls you want are there. You'll then have to decide how to handle decisions going forward.

What if the two of you can't agree on what the tech rules should be for your kids? This is especially fraught when you're divorced and/or coparenting. Those decisions should be handled just like any other important parenting decisions. Don't assume your fellow parent agrees with you—have the conversation. It might not be an easy one, but it's crucial to discuss issues around devices.

TRACKING

One thing we haven't yet discussed is tracking your kid's location. To track or not to track?

If you've made it this far, you know that giving your kid a smartphone just so you can track them is a bad idea. Parents sometimes do this thinking their kid will be safer, but then the phone takes over the kid's life and the kid is actually less safe because of what they are experiencing online and what they are not experiencing in the real world.

If your kid is 16 and has their driver's license, using the iPhone "Find My Friends" tracking or the Android equivalent is tempting. We used it for K, mostly because she was gone so often her last two years of high school and it was nice to see where she was instead of having to text her "Where are you?" It's more for convenience than safety.

Still, my family calls Find My Friends "the stalker app." That shows our ambivalence about it. Like most Gen Xers, I was very glad my parents didn't know exactly where I was at every second during my senior year in high school. Let Grow founder Lenore Skenazy, who advocates for child and teen independence, wrote on X, "Many folks today have come to believe that tracking—a non-possibility for all of human history till now—is now a 'must' for safety's sake. It is not! It is a must for building anxiety in parents (who start to think they have to watch their kids at all times) and kids (who grow up thinking it is normal never to have a moment they are not under adult surveillance, life is just THAT dangerous, and they are just THAT incompetent)."

Here's a good middle ground. If using the stalker app means you'll be more likely to let your older teen do something independent (like drive a long distance for the first time), then have it on. But once they've done that and they are making their way toward more maturity, turn it off.

Once they are off to college or living independently, definitely turn it off. After a talk I gave at a college parent weekend, an 18-year-old student and her parents asked me if I thought they should turn tracking off on her phone. "I had to take my roommate to the hospital and my parents called me freaking out," the student said. "And when I go to a party, I don't exactly want them to know that." I told her parents to turn it off: time to stop the stalking.

COMMON OBSTACLES AND PUSHBACKS

1. **Won't my kid just find work-arounds for parental controls?** They might. I've heard lots of stories about this, so it's worth being aware of. This is why it's essential to have several lines of defense instead of just one (for example, no phones in the bedroom overnight *and* using the Downtime setting; not giving your kid a phone that can have social media until 16).

   Work-arounds mostly happen for time limits. For example, a kid will change the time zone of their iPhone so they can continue to use it late at night. To prevent this, get your kid's phone (yeah, I know) and go to Settings > Screen Time > Content & Privacy Restrictions > Location Services > System Services > Setting Time Zone—and turn that off. Then go back to Location Services and set to "Don't Allow Changes." (This is a great example of how cumbersome operating system parental controls are.) Fortunately, it's much harder for kids to get around app download blocks or disallowed websites. Third-party software is also harder for kids to circumvent.

2. **I've blocked or limited social media/gaming for my kid, and now they're having a meltdown. Help!** If they're having a meltdown, they're probably addicted or at least overly attached. That means you did the right thing. The first few days, maybe the first week, will be rough. Then they will slowly learn how to live without being glued to a gaming console or a phone for hours and hours a day. Don't give in during those first difficult days. It will get better, and by the second week you should see considerable improvement.

   There's also the question of cold turkey (a total ban on the activity right away) versus time limits. Start with limits. For example, if they've been gaming every waking minute, set a limit of an hour a day. If they won't respect the limit or you don't see an improvement in attitude or behavior after a week, tell them the other option is a total ban. That can be a motivator for respecting limits. And if limits don't change their behavior or mood, go cold turkey with a total ban. The first few days will be tough, but within a week you'll get your kid back.

3. **Shouldn't kids learn how to manage their phone use on their own?** Not when porn and social media sites don't verify age, and not when they're not mature enough to manage their own use—after all, many adults struggle to manage their phone use. You can loosen some parental controls as your kids get older and they have demonstrated that they

can use their phone or laptop responsibly. Even with parental controls, your kid will get plenty of practice managing their phone use within the limits you set. Even better, they will build good habits. It will be normal to them to put their devices away at bedtime, for example.

4. **If kids don't learn how to manage their own use when they are young, won't they go crazy when the controls are lifted?** Probably not—when the controls are lifted (at 16, 18, or whatever), they will be more mature and better able to handle their tech use. They'll also be at an age when they have more options for getting together with friends as they will have their driver's license or be able to take public transportation on their own. Plus, the parental controls outlined in this chapter are not all-or-nothing extremes. Under these controls kids still learn how to use technology, but with reasonable guardrails in place.

RULE 7: CREATE NO-PHONE ZONES

We were on the snorkel boat when I realized my mistake.

Against the stunningly green backdrop of Hawaii's Big Island, 17-year-old K was standing on the boat deck talking on her smartphone to one of her friends back home. During a family trip we'd planned for months. And no, it wasn't an emergency.

As family fails go, it was minor. No one was physically hurt. It didn't disrupt our travel plans. Unlike when J somehow misplaced all of her 6th-grade textbooks, it didn't cost us any money.

But it still didn't feel right, and it wasn't the only time tech intruded on our trip. The next evening, K pulled out her phone to answer texts while we were deep in conversation. During the entire trip, the instant her phone vibrated, she took it out of her pocket. We'd done so much to keep her away from digital media until she was ready, but technology was still interfering in our lives. She wasn't fully present on one of our last trips as a family before she went to college.

As I learned the hard way on this trip, there are places where phones don't belong, especially for kids and teens. Sometimes that's about their being present in the moment; other times it's about having time away from devices when they can play outside, wind down before sleep, or read.

Here are a few times that should be no-phone zones, or at least involve minimal access to devices:

1. **The hour (or at least the half hour) before bedtime.** As you saw in Rule 2, kids who use devices in bed before they go to sleep don't sleep as well or as long. The same is true of adults: College students who used devices for an hour before bed were 59% more likely to have symptoms of insomnia and slept 24 minutes less than those who didn't use devices before bed. That's mostly because electronic devices stimulate the brain, which is the opposite of what you want before going to bed, when you instead want to calm the brain down. Teens know this. "For certain apps, like TikTok, it's really hard to fall asleep once you use it close to when you're gonna go to sleep," said a 10th grader. "I can't use it within an hour, or else I'd struggle . . . and then I'll just get back on the app 'cause I'm not sleeping anyway."

   Going to sleep is like landing a plane: It can't be done suddenly. Instead, it takes at least 30 minutes to wind down for sleep. A half hour or (even better) an hour before bed, kids should be doing something relaxing. That means no social media, texting, internet surfing, gaming, or homework, none of which are relaxing. This is a great rule for adults to follow as well—try it, and you'll sleep better.

If kids are reading before bed, they should be reading a physical book or on a Kindle or other e-reader, not on a laptop or tablet. Laptops and tablets are backlit, so they create blue light that prevents the brain from making the sleep hormone melatonin. These devices are also brimming with distractions, making it very tempting to stop reading and check out the latest video on YouTube or open Canvas to see if your teacher has updated your grades. There are just too many things to do on these devices for them to be relaxing. In contrast, e-readers like the Kindle do just one thing. They also have black-and-white screens that look more like paper. Make sure your kid has the backlight turned off when they are reading at night; they should read with external light, like a lamp, that doesn't shine directly into the eyes. Even better, they can read a physical book.

What about TV or streaming? These are more passive, so they are a better choice than other screen activities for the time before bed. Ideally, kids should be watching shows on a traditional TV, not on a laptop, tablet, or phone where, again, there are too many distractions. Plus laptops, tablets, and phones are held close to the face, exposing the eyes to more blue light than a TV across the room. (And remember, the TV they use should *not* be in their bedroom.)

Even then, TVs do emit blue light. The solution is to wear orange safety glasses, which filter out blue light. You can buy them online for about $18. You'll look like a welder wearing pajamas, but you (and your kid) will fall asleep faster and sleep better.

2. **Family dinner.** Have you ever been out at a restaurant and seen a family sitting together at a table not talking to each other, each looking down at their own device? It's extremely common, but it shouldn't be. Family dinners, whether at home or in a restaurant, should be a no-phone zone. That goes for the adults, too. This is your time to have a face-to-face conversation without the distractions of technology. When social psychologists randomly assigned people to have dinner with friends or family with or without their phone accessible, those without their phones enjoyed the dinner more.

   It's even more important to have device-free dinner if you have guests or go to a relative's house. In many families, there are a limited number of times when your kids can talk to their grandparents, aunts, uncles, or cousins, and that precious time shouldn't be interrupted by devices.

3. **Face-to-face conversations.** If you're going to talk about anything in depth, phones should be set aside or left in another room. Having a deep conversation is very difficult when phones keep buzzing and the flow is constantly interrupted. Experiments find that setting phones aside during everyday conversations results in an even larger increase in enjoyment and happiness than phone-free dinners.

   There's actually a word for taking out a phone while talking to someone else: *phubbing* (it's a combination of *phone* and *snubbing*). Everyone hates phubbing, even though it seems like everyone also does it. Suggest that your kids talk about phubbing with their friends—that when they're together in person, to leave their phones in another room for (say) thirty minutes. Then they don't have to worry about their friend taking out their phone when they're talking or wondering if their friend is really paying attention or if they're boring. As a general rule, kids and teens don't mind putting their phones away for a time as long as everyone does it.

4. **Vacations.** After the experience in Hawaii, I made a decision: On our next trip, I was taking away our children's phones. I bought them each a digital camera so they could capture their own pictures without having to use their phones. I got a little pushback, mostly from K, but not as much as I'd feared. And it was glorious: We talked. They looked out the window at the natural wonders around them. They laughed. They were *there*. I'm taking away phones for family vacations from now on. And if they want to keep up their Duolingo streak, they can use my laptop.

   What about long car and plane rides? For some kids, it makes sense to make an exception for transportation time, especially on planes. Once kids are about eight, though, plane rides are also a good time to get them to read, and—let's face it—that's only going to happen if they don't have the option of watching movies.

5. **Camp and outside time.** Consider sending your kids to a no-screens-allowed outdoor camp, either a day camp or an overnight camp. They will be outside and interacting with people face-to-face without the temptation of being on a device. The best part: You won't have to argue with them about it. Let's hear it for outsourcing!

My kids have gone to a camp in San Diego called Outpost since K was in kindergarten. Their motto is "Outside and Unplugged." Especially as my kids got older, sending them to camp meant fewer summer days I had to keep them off screens.

Camps can be expensive, but research has definitively shown their benefits. After 6th graders spent five days at an outdoor camp without screen devices, their social skills were better than their peers who hadn't gone to camp yet. Teens who spent two weeks at a Scout camp developed more self-control, empathy, and self-confidence.

It's important to choose a camp where kids spend most of the time outside. Barring that, it should be a camp where they interact with other people face-to-face. Think theater camp yes, coding camp no. Academic camps where kids sit in classrooms don't give kids a break from the school year and often involve, yep, more screens. It's tempting to enroll them in an academic camp to give them a leg up in school, but resist the urge—kids need outdoor time with sunshine and physical activity, and summer is the best time to get that—and yes, that goes for middle- and high-school-age kids as well.

Any outside time is great. Gen Z teens have come up with a very cogent piece of advice for their chronically online peers: "Go touch grass." In other words, put down the phone and go outside. Find ways for your kids to do this apart from going to camp. If you have a backyard, push your kids into it. If you don't have a yard, allow them to walk to the park as long as they're old enough (about eight) and responsible enough. Yes, they'll be fine, and no, you don't have to track them. Biking is also a great way for kids to get outside and explore their neighborhood (more in Rule 8).

6. **Summer or weekend downtime.** If your kids have downtime over the summer when they're not in camp, have a no-screens or limited-screens rule. During the school year, kids are doing their homework on laptops, so it's tough to carve out tech-free times. Every summer, I take E and J's laptops. They can have a limited amount of laptop time (no more than an hour a day) to do specific things. The rest of the time, they can come up with something else to do. Last summer, that meant riding their bikes around the neighborhood, jumping on the trampoline, and reading books. Invariably, they won't do those things if screen time is available. One technique to get kids thinking is to invite them to list 25 things they would do if screens didn't exist. Then when they don't have screens available they have a handy list of other things they can do.

   I'll admit it: One of my main motivations for taking my kids' laptops is to try to get them to read. As a college professor, I routinely meet smart kids who have read very few books before they get to college. They have little idea how to focus their attention for longer than a few minutes and have trouble succeeding in college courses that require reading textbooks, novels, or even long magazine articles. As an *Atlantic* article recently put it, "To read a book in college, it helps if you read a book in high school." In recent years, 40% of high school seniors have not read a single book in the last year that wasn't assigned for school.

Back in the early 1980s, that was true of only 15% of high school seniors.

This isn't just a problem for academic preparation. Novels teach empathy and an understanding of the human condition. Especially for complex issues, nonfiction books give a more in-depth and informed view than YouTube shorts can. Reading things longer than a brief web article is an important life skill.

When K was nine, she stayed with me at a lake cabin for a week after the rest of the family had gone home. I had tried in vain to get her to read voluntarily for years, but she was one of those kids who didn't like to sit still. But I told her I'd be working, so she had to find something else to do. Without her sisters to play with, she got bored very quickly. She read the Minnesota fishing guide regulations and then moved on to the one book she'd brought with her. When she finished it, she asked for the next in the series, so I got it delivered. That finally got her to love reading, and these days her favorite book is *And the Band Played On* by Randy Shilts, a history of the AIDS epidemic that's 660 pages long. She's now in college and considering majoring in public health.

To get your kids reading, have lots of magazines and books around the house—if it's on the coffee table they might reach for a magazine instead of their phone. Make an outing of going to the library or the bookstore. Have reading challenges with prizes (like: If you read three books this month, you get . . . that toy you want, to pick out dessert for a week, etc.). Take books with you when you visit the doctor's office, go on a trip, or head anywhere you might have downtime.

COMMON OBSTACLES AND PUSHBACKS

1. **"But I have to have my phone [right before bed, during this conversation, etc.] because my friends will be mad at me otherwise."** Many kids, especially teens, pull out their phones every time they buzz, because they are afraid they will miss a text or call from a friend—and then their friend will assume they're mad at them. Suggest that they talk to their friends about this directly. They can say "Sometimes I'm doing homework or talking to my parents, so I won't text you back right away. It doesn't mean I'm mad at you." With the instant text response now a social norm, it's a necessary conversation, and their friends will understand. Many teens quietly admit they like getting a break from their phones and the expectation of the instant response.

2. **"But I need my laptop during the summer/break for [shopping, reading about an interest, etc.]"** That's what the hour a day is for. Using third-party parental controls (see Rules 6 and 9) is the best way to enforce this—it will shut down the device after the hour is up. Alternatively, you can tell them they have to give it back to you after an hour or they lose the next day's time. The downside of a time limit is most kids will use all of the time even if they don't really need it. But I still think that's better than hours and hours spent on a screen when they could be doing other things.

3. **"But, Mom, I'm bored."** Your reply could be something like this: "Great! Use that feeling to find something interesting to do."

Also share this with them: Using your device is not going to cure your boredom. In fact, it's going to make it worse. In one experiment, people who had their phones available during conversations with friends were more likely to say they were bored than those who did not have their phones available. So it's not just that boredom leads to device use—device use also leads to boredom.

At first this seems counterintuitive, but it makes sense: Device time is just not as interesting or as meaningful as what's going on in the real world. Everything teens do in the real world is linked to less boredom, and everything they do on devices is linked to more boredom (see Figure 7.1).

Trying to avoid boredom is one reason why people often quickly switch between apps or videos on their devices.

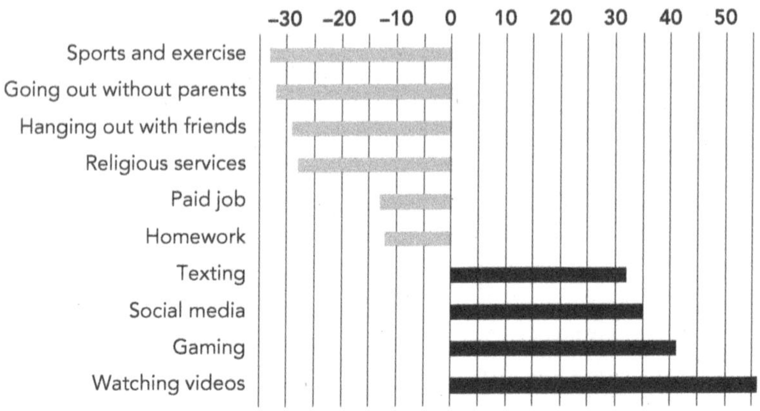

Figure 7.1: Increase or decrease in risk of being bored, screen and non-screen activities

Source: Monitoring the Future survey of 8th and 10th graders

Note: Controlled for sex, race/ethnicity, grade, and mother's education level. Black bars are screen device activities; gray bars are activities that do not involve a screen. Compares teens who spend more time on the activity versus less.

However, it doesn't work: In a series of experiments, digital app switching led to more boredom, not less. It also caused people to feel less meaning in the moment. Online time is so often empty calories.

More time on devices might be one of the reasons why more and more teens say they are bored. In 2008, when few teens had smartphones, 45% of 8th graders said they were often bored. By 2023, it was 61%. Devices filled with bite-size videos were supposed to mean we were never bored, but instead more teens than ever are filled with ennui.

What should they do instead? Go touch grass.

RULE 8: GIVE YOUR KIDS REAL-WORLD FREEDOM

When UK journalist Decca Aitkenhead decided to write an article on the impact of smartphones, she started at home. She asked her two sons, ages 13 and 14, and a group of their friends to trade their smartphones for Light Phones for a month. She then added an extra twist: What would happen if they went on an unsupervised and smartphone-free campout for a night?

Nothing good, according to the staff at her newspaper, who freaked out over safety concerns and came close to nixing the idea. But the kids' parents signed waivers, and eventually the kids took the Tube, a train, a bus, and walked a two-mile trail to their camping location, the wild and wooded grounds of a 16th-century manor house deep in rural Kent.

Aitkenhead doubted the trip would be very exciting since all of the kids had camped before with their parents. But upon arriving the next day, she wrote, "The mood is electric," with the teens gushing about how much fun they had, how they loved the campfire, how they played guitar and chased one another around in the dark. How much difference would it have made, Aitkenhead asks her 14-year-old son, if she had come with them on the train and camped nearby? "I would have hated it," he says through clenched teeth. "Hated every single second."

It's a typical teenage response—teens want to hang out with their friends and build their independence outside the watchful (and lame) gazes of adults. In today's culture, though, they get fewer chances to do that than their parents' generation did as teens.

It begins in childhood. While 10-year-olds once had the free range of their neighborhoods, many kids these days are not allowed to go anywhere by themselves. Half of 5- to 14-year-olds used to walk or bike to school by themselves; now only one in 10 do. While 13 was once considered old enough to be a babysitter, many now think 13-year-olds need a babysitter.

When older Gen Xers were the 13- and 14-year-olds in 8th grade, in the early 1990s, most earned some money during the school year and about half went out on dates. Now only about one in four kids that age do either. By the time teens reach their senior year of high school, at age 17 or 18, fewer have their driver's license, go out on dates, or work at paid jobs than in previous generations (see Figure 8.1 on the following page).

If you want to get Gen Xers and older Millennials to open up online, just mention how unsupervised we were growing up. "Parents had literally no idea where their kids were or what they were doing like 90% of the time," wrote Shannon Foley Martinez. Another said, "I roamed far and wide from age 4 onward. . . . I wasn't neglected and I'm thankful my parents

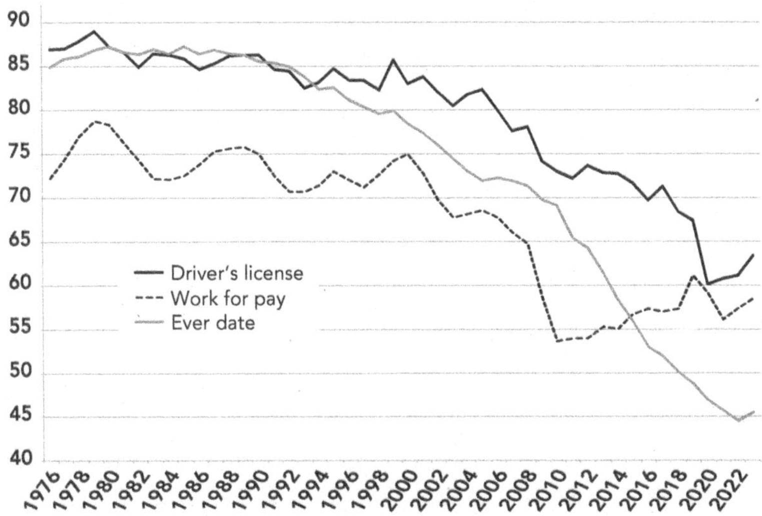

Figure 8.1: Percent of U.S. 12th graders who have a driver's license, work for pay, or ever date, 1976–2023

Source: Monitoring the Future survey

didn't hover over my life as if I were made of glass." A third wrote, "Parents in the 80s had to be reminded that they even had children . . . Gen X played outside until the streetlights came on [and] drank water from a hose . . . [we were] the Feral Generation." TV ads that ran between the 1960s and 1990s asked parents, "It's 10 p.m. Do you know where your children are?" Often, the answer was no, no they didn't—especially if their kids were teens.

Not all of this was good—back then, a lot more teens drank alcohol and had sex, for example. But when they went off to college or got their first job, they'd already had plenty of experience with independence and decision-making. College students didn't call their parents every time they had an issue; they solved it themselves. No one had yet decided that the word *adult* needed to be a verb (as in *adulting*)—or required lessons.

Things are different now. Eighteen-year-olds are scared to make phone calls. When college students fight with their roommates, their parents step in and call the school. Young adults take their parents to job interviews. A manager once told me about a young employee who invited her father to her annual job performance review.

How did this happen? Over the last few decades, we have under-protected kids in the digital world while over-protecting them in the physical world, leaving them unprepared for adulthood. Letting kids and teens have more freedom corrects that imbalance. More real-world freedom is also the answer to an essential question: If kids aren't using devices as much, what are they supposed to do with all of that time?

How about what you probably did most of your childhood and teen years: hang out with friends in person, ride bikes, play, do projects, and yes, get bored? When you were a teen, you might have babysat younger kids, worked at the mall, driven around with your friends, or mowed lawns. In *The Anxious Generation*, Jonathan Haidt argues that the play- and independence-based childhood has been replaced by the phone-based childhood. If we're going to cut back on the phone-based childhood, we have to get our kids back to play and independence. Or, to put it another way: take away the tablet and open the door.

That does not mean travel soccer. It doesn't even mean Y soccer. Kids need a wide swath of time when they are calling the shots, not adults. That's how they develop social skills, creativity, and problem-solving ability. These are the things they need to become competent adults, and many kids today aren't getting them. As psychologist Peter Gray has noted, when adults and kids are together, the adults are the adults and the kids are kids. It's only when adults aren't around that kids start to become adults.

I'll let you in on a secret: When kids are more independent, your job as a parent becomes easier. You do fewer things for your kids and gain back time to work, relax, or whatever. It's a win-win situation. One reason parents today are so stressed is because they're spending more time than ever with their kids. And one reason kids today are so stressed is . . . the same thing. Both generations need more time apart.

When kids do things on their own—anything from tying their own shoes to going on camping trips to getting a job—they are learning. Once parents recognize that, it's a lot easier to let go. One study found that when parents hear that independent activities are teachable moments, they intervene only half as much. Letting go is not irresponsible parenting. It's the opposite—it's enriching. So how can we help our kids learn independence? We'll start with ideas for kids 3 to 12 and then move on to building independence among teens.

HELPING KIDS 3 TO 12 DEVELOP INDEPENDENCE

The key for this age group is for kids to play and do things on their own (walk to school, read for fun, run errands, cook) without adults hovering over them. This way, they can develop skills to contribute to the family. One of the best parenting books I've ever read is *Hunt, Gather, Parent*, by NPR science reporter

Michaeleen Doucleff. Learning about parenting techniques from more traditional cultures helped Doucleff be a better parent to her then-three-year-old daughter Rosy. In the Indigenous families she visited, Doucleff noticed, toddlers loved to help out. They don't think of this as "doing chores." They think of it as taking their place in the world—being a helpful, competent part of the team they love: their family. Doucleff also learned that if this desire is not met—if the child has few or zero opportunities to help make dinner, bathe the baby, wash the dishes—the desire to help actually "extinguishes." Who wants that? So Doucleff cut way back on child-centered activities and let Rosy do things around the house like sweeping and helping cook, without too much correction or interference or even teaching on Doucleff's part. Throughout human history, kids have learned by observing, copying, and trying things, far more than by direct instruction. When Rosy became a productive member of the family, her behavior improved.

Another key piece: It's important not to cave when kids say they are scared to do something. The most effective cure for anxiety is experience. A lot of things are scary until you do them. Then they're not scary anymore. Many kids are scared to do things on their own because they simply never have. This can intensify when kids believe their *parents* think they can't handle a new situation. The official name for having people do things they are scared of is exposure therapy. Even people with severe phobias can be cured by slowly (or quickly!) being exposed to the source of their fears. They make it through the experience, nothing terrible happens, and their anxiety dissipates. If kids are going to develop independence and resilience, they are going to have to do things that initially scare them a little.

In fact, independence is being tested as treatment for kids with diagnosed anxiety disorders. One study had clinically anxious kids do new things on their own almost every day for four weeks—things that the kids (anxious though they were) wanted to do, and that their parents (anxious though *they* were) were prompted by the researcher to allow. So the kids went to the store, rode public transit, walked to school, hung out at the park, and so on. Result? They went from feeling worried "most of the time" to feeling worried "a little bit of the time." That's a huge change. And note that this did not just transform the child—the parents were proud and happy, too.

A great organization advocating for kids' independence is called Let Grow. Its mission statement says, in part, "We believe today's kids are smarter and stronger than our culture gives them credit for. We reject the idea that they are in constant physical, emotional or psychological danger from creeps, kidnapping, frustration, failure, baby snatchers, bad grades, disappointing playdates and/or the perils of a non-organic grape." Let Grow has free independence-building programs and materials for families and schools. Giving your kids real-world freedom means stepping back so the kids can step up. Parental worries go down as kids do more and more.

Here are a few concrete ideas for getting out of kids' way and helping them build independence:

1. **Do it yourself, kiddo.** One pretty universal principle for parenting kids a year old and up: If they can do it themselves, let them do it themselves. Even young children can get dressed and put their shoes on by themselves. (Yes, it's going to take longer, but they will get faster the more they

do it.) If they spill something, they should clean it up. If they drop something, they should pick it up. If they take out their toys, they should put them back. When kids are about 8 to 10 years old, they can do their own laundry.

When my kids were younger, they would frequently say, "Mom, can you [get me a cup / make me some cereal / open the door]?" Much of the time, I would answer, "No, but you can." Sometimes that came from having three kids and not enough hands. But I also realized it was a good answer for them developing independence. Try putting the kid cups on a lower shelf and buying smaller cartons of milk that are easier for little hands to pour.

2. **Grocery shopping.** When you go shopping with your four- to seven-year-old kids, ask them to go get something for you that's a few aisles away. Start by telling them where to find it. ("Can you go get us some mac and cheese? It's in the next aisle that way.") Later, you can just tell them to find the item. They'll find it eventually—and learn they can figure things out themselves. In a 2023 poll, only 50% of parents of kids ages 9 to 11 have had them do this! So if your kid can do this at seven, they'll be ahead of the game.

   Once kids are in third grade or so, most are ready to go into a store or quick-serve restaurant themselves and buy something. If you're in the suburbs, that can mean waiting in the parking lot while your kid goes inside. If you're in a city, it might mean your kid walking a few blocks to a neighborhood store. (Fun fact: Kids can use your credit card and sign their own name—you don't have to give them cash. Just make sure to discuss how much they are allowed to spend.)

K, our oldest, asked to do things like this by the time she was nine, and loved feeling independent by running into the grocery store to grab a few items or ordering a burger by herself. Perhaps as a result, she adapted easily when she got her driver's license at 16 and started spending more time out of the house.

Our younger two, though, were more reluctant. When J was 12, I realized with a start she'd never gone into a store by herself. So one spring break when the rest of the family was out of town, I told her we could get some special snacks we didn't usually buy. That sounded good to her. Then I told her she would have to go into the store and buy them herself. She instantly said, "I'm not doing that." I shrugged and said, "OK, but then we're not getting the special snacks." She thought about it for a minute and said, "Does it have to be a grocery store? Can it be Target?" I said that was fine. "Can I use the self-checkout? Because talking to the cashier might be cringe." Yes, I said. "Can I have two credit cards in case the first one doesn't work?" Sure, no problem.

So I gave her two credit cards and sat in the car in the parking lot as she headed into the store on her own. Ten minutes later, she was back, with Lucky Charms, lemonade, and Doritos. Her review? "That was easy." It's true—the best cure for anxiety is experience.

3. **Go places on their own.** When Let Grow founder Lenore Skenazy's son was nine, he begged her to let him take the New York subway by himself. She gave him a MetroCard,

some money, and a subway map and left him in Ladies' Handbags at Bloomingdales (because that department sits over the subway stop). An hour later he was home safe—and thrilled.

When Skenazy wrote about her son's adventure in a newspaper column, she was quickly labeled "America's Worst Mom." But she realized she was onto something—kids wanted the independence their parents had enjoyed when they were young, and kids weren't getting it even though the world was actually safer. She ended up writing the extremely useful (and hilarious) book *Free-Range Kids: How to Let Go and Let Grow*. She then cofounded Let Grow (along with Jonathan Haidt and Peter Gray) to advocate for children's independence.

What this means for your family: It's fine for kids to walk or bike to school, a friend's house, or the park—with the appropriate calculation of age versus distance (the older they are, they farther they can go). Isn't this dangerous? Not really. Crime is lower now than it was when Gen Xers were wandering around their neighborhoods until the streetlights came on. (Also see the first three "Common obstacles and pushbacks" at the end of the chapter.) Of course, it makes sense to factor in the realities of your own town or neighborhood.

What about well-meaning strangers who will assume your child is abandoned? On the Let Grow website, parents can download a "Kid License" kids can carry that has their parent's name, signature, and phone number and says "I am not lost or neglected! I've got permission to be out here—feel free to call!" Let Grow has also helped pass Reasonable Childhood Independence laws in eight states, with more states considering such laws. These laws say that "neglect" is when you put your child in obvious, serious danger—not anytime you take your eyes off them.

Having kids fly alone is also a great experience. Children can fly without a parent starting at age five (!) when you pay for the unaccompanied minor service. K flew alone starting at age seven and loved it. When she was 12, she flew on a connecting flight from her friend's house in Maryland to meet us for a family trip to Minnesota—and without the unaccompanied minor service since Southwest Airlines allows kids 12 and over to fly independently. She even transferred between terminals at the Minneapolis airport, all on her own. She talked about that experience with pride for years. Which is, by the way, how you know that independence is more than just "nice." It is formative. That's why most of us remember the first time we did something on our own—took a trip, got a babysitting gig, even when we got lost or screwed up and handled it ourselves. All of those are huge milestones. And exposure therapy!

4. **Take care of pets.** Walking the dog is an especially good task for kids—they're not only taking care of their pet but also getting the chance to walk in the neighborhood independently. Kids can also be responsible for feeding pets and cleaning the cat's litterbox or the guinea pig or hamster cage starting at quite a young age.

5. **Drop them off.** When we were kids, our parents would drop us off at the mall, the movie theater, the ice cream shop, the pizza parlor, the skating rink, the park, or the amusement

park with our friends and come back for us after a few hours (or sometimes the whole day). Do this with your kids when they're ready (often somewhere between eight and 10). For malls and amusement parks, be sure to check out the policies about kids being there on their own. Some don't allow it; others do during the day but not at night.

6. **Stay at home alone.** Most kids are ready to be at home alone for a few hours by age seven or so. It's common to think, "What if something happens?" But really, what's going to happen, assuming your kid is not a pyromaniac? They'll be fine. It's good if they have access to a phone, one reason to have a landline if you can. Flip phones and smartwatches are also great for this.

7. **Go to camp.** Camp is already a good idea for non-screen outdoor time, but it also builds independence in a safe environment. Sleepaway camp in particular builds autonomy in kids as they learn how to do things without their parents around. All three of my kids went to sleepaway camp before age 10, and they always came home with more confidence.

8. **Sleep over at a friend's house.** Kids get more time in person with friends and time away from their own parents, helping them be more independent. Start small, with just two friends getting together. Yes, have a conversation with the parents about potential safety risks (allergies, guns in the home, a pool in the backyard). But then let them go. As Erika Christakis wrote in *The Atlantic*, "denying our

children a chance to learn up close from other families shortchanges children's autonomy. . . . Why does it matter if our kids eat junk food for a night, or hear unwelcome political views, or sit through the wrong kind of prayers (or no prayers) at dinnertime? . . . Sleepovers, for all of their flaws, humanized others, and as a result, they made me more human too."

9. **Cook.** Most kids can start helping with the non-stove parts of cooking as preschoolers and can cook on their own after that. To start where their interests lie, brownies or cupcakes from a mix are an easy and yummy first experience. Next, they can learn how to make pasta or heat up a frozen pizza. Then move on to making a more complicated (and healthier) entrée for dinner, and then a whole meal. Have your kids help you cook a meal, and the next time they can do it themselves without assistance. Bonus: Then you don't have to cook that night.

10. **Do household chores.** Give kids the job of emptying the dishwasher, taking out the trash, or mowing the lawn once they're old enough. They should also be making their own lunches by the time they're eight or so. And pro tip: no need to call any of this a "chore." Your kids are part of a team—your family—and naturally everyone pitches in.

11. **Make phone calls.** Many college students tell me they are afraid to make phone calls—they never did it growing up and now it seems intimidating. Have your kids do this as much as possible. Younger kids can call Grandma on

their own. Older kids can call in a food takeout or delivery order.

12. **Play outside, build stuff, etc.** Anything that kids can do on their own is a good idea. The Let Grow website has a free "Independence Kit" with a long list of other activities parents and children can consider. (A sample: "Frisbee! Tag! Frisbee Tag!" "Build something you can use.") Giving your kids a digital camera (see Rule 7) also works well here—kids can spend hours taking pictures and videos around the house, in the backyard, and at the park.

HELPING TEENS 13 TO 18 DEVELOP INDEPENDENCE

A few years ago, I met Priya, a 14-year-old high school freshman. When I asked her what she did for fun with her friends, she said she went to the movies. "Do your parents drop you off?" I asked, remembering my own pre–driver's license teen years in the 1980s when my friends and I would enjoy a few parent-free hours. No, she said, "usually one parent comes along, or two." They find a movie everyone will like, she said, and the parents and children go together—just as they did when the kids were in elementary school.

Priya's experience is not unusual anymore. Teens are not going out without their parents as much as they used to (see Figure 8.2 on the following page). Even high school seniors, most of whom have a driver's license, are sticking closer to home and closer to parents these days. They go out about as often as 8th graders—four years younger—did a decade prior.

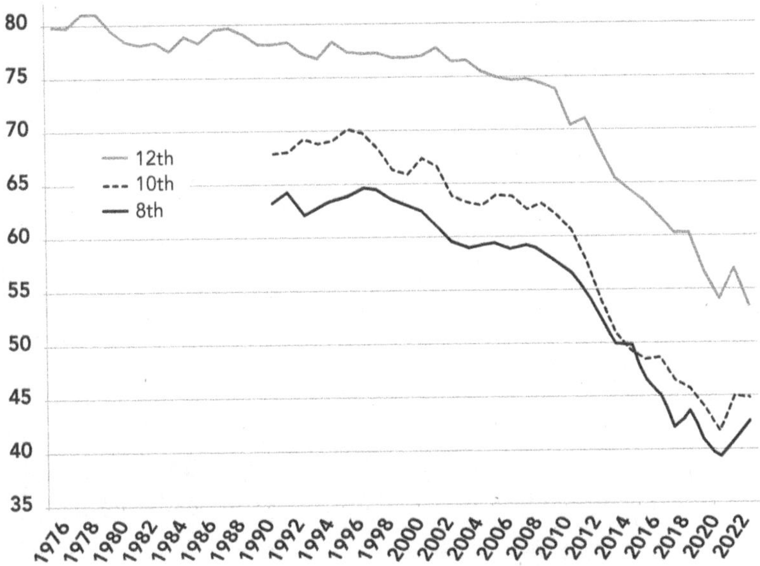

Figure 8.2: Percent of U.S. teens who go out with friends (and without parents) two or more times a week, 1976–2023

Source: Monitoring the Future survey

Some of the decline in going out is because of phones and social media—why go out on a Saturday night when you can stay in your room and Snapchat with your friends instead? Putting it that way makes you realize how sad it actually is.

Some teens don't want to go out on their own because they didn't do it as children, so are now scared to do it as teens. Many parents are pleased their teens are staying at home instead of going out with their friends and doing who knows what. Or they forbid their teens from going out, citing safety concerns.

It's true teens are less likely to get in a car accident if they're not going out as much—you could argue that they are physically safer this way, even though risks are very low. But are they mentally safer? No—it's the opposite. Eighth graders are less likely to be depressed when they go out, spend time with friends in person, attend religious services, or exercise—all things in the real world. But they are more likely to be depressed if they spend more time with devices. The same link appears for 10th graders: Those who go out, date, and drive are happier than those who don't.

So what can parents do?

1. **Up the expectations, especially for life skills.** Go to the list in the previous section on kids and independence and take each to the next level. At 13 almost all kids can walk or bike three miles by themselves, if not farther. Teens can be expected to cook dinner for the family once or twice a week, do their own laundry, or do yard work. They should be making phone calls, too. Once they can get places on their own, they can grocery shop by themselves as well. Kids 13 and up can certainly be dropped off at the mall, the movies, or the pizza place to spend time with their friends away from adults. They can also babysit younger kids.

2. **Get them a bike or, if you can afford it, an e-bike.** In my neighborhood in northern San Diego, e-bikes have given 11- to 15-year-olds newfound freedom. Kids can get to school, stores, and friends' houses on their own. Regular bikes can also expand the independence of this age group. Obviously, this privilege is for kids who can be trusted to follow traffic laws. Have them take an e-bike safety course,

and don't forget the helmet. If your kid is reluctant, they can start with short jaunts around the block before venturing farther.

3. **Encourage the driver's license.** Yes, it's scary to think that your kid who was in kindergarten just a decade ago is going to get behind the wheel of a car. But in a lot of neighborhoods, it's the key to independence. Put your fears aside and do what you can to help your teen get their license, even if they are scared to do so. (Exposure therapy! For them *and* you!) Using Rule 5 (no smartphone until you get your driver's license) is another way to nudge reluctant teens toward driving. If you're in a big city, the equivalent is getting around on public transportation, which most kids can do by fourth grade or so. (In Tokyo, kids start taking the subway in 1st grade, suggesting kids are ready for this long before our culture assumes.) Once they can get around by themselves, teens can do all kinds of things independently, from seeing friends to going to concerts or sporting events.

4. **Flying or taking a train alone.** If your kid hasn't flown or taken a long-distance train alone yet, and you have the means and opportunity, set it up. Teens can take Amtrak trains alone starting at 13 as long as a caregiver signs a waiver and they're met by an adult at their destination. At 16 they can travel completely on their own on Amtrak. For flights, you can pay for the unaccompanied minor service until teens turn 18 or have them travel without it (when they can do that varies by airline: on Southwest it's 12; on

Alaska Airlines it's 13; on most other airlines it's 15). Even reluctant kids can shine doing this. E is the definition of reluctant, but when she was 14 she met me in New York by taking an Alaska Airlines flight without the unaccompanied minor service. She was nervous, but afterward said, "Actually, that was really easy." As I write this, she's 15 and on a flight by herself to visit her cousins in Minnesota, having negotiated a long security line on her own.

5. **Making appointments.** Have your teen make their own doctor, dentist, and haircut appointments. That gets them in charge of their own calendars, something they will need to do when they go to college. Once they're driving or taking public transport alone, they can also go to the appointments by themselves. One less thing on Mom or Dad's schedule! The doctor's office may call you to get your consent to treat your child—that's what happened when K started going to appointments by herself at 16. But that was a lot less time-consuming than taking her to the appointment myself.

6. **Jobs and volunteer work.** Whether it's paid or volunteer, the responsibility of having a job really helps kids grow up. The camp my kids go to has a junior counselor program for high school students where they help out the college-age senior counselors with the younger kids. They're not paid, but parents also don't have to pay to send them. K was a junior counselor for three summers. She'd come home with all kinds of crazy stories about what the campers did—and how she had to figure out how to handle it. Some of the

campers became very attached to her. Most of all, she felt useful. That's exactly what teens need, and they usually don't get that feeling of usefulness from doing schoolwork. If getting a job with set hours is not in the cards, babysitting, mowing lawns, taking in neighbors' trash cans, or helping out older neighbors or relatives are all useful jobs.

7. **Walking, hiking, camping.** Gen Z is surprisingly self-aware about their tech addictions—thus their advice to "Go touch grass." Touching grass can be combined with independence when teens go for a hike or go to a park with friends—and without adults. Camping trips, like the one Decca Aitkenhead set up for her sons and their friends, are also great.

8. **Learning how to handle money.** When K first got her driver's license, we loaned her a credit card. A credit card statement full of fast-food charges later, we realized our mistake. We then set up a proxy bank account for her and transferred $50 a week to it. We figured that was fair since she drove herself and her sister to school. The key was she had a limited amount left after she paid for gas—not a blank check. We could have also given her $50 in cash a week, but we figured putting it in an account where she could use a debit card was easier.

COMMON OBSTACLES AND PUSHBACKS

1. **"But the world is such a dangerous place now."** Except it's not. Crime is *lower* now than it was when most parents were kids in the 1970s–1990s. Stranger kidnappings are

exceedingly rare—it's more likely your kid will be struck by lightning than kidnapped by a stranger. But aren't there "a lot of creeps out there"? There are some, but there aren't any more than when you were a kid. There may even be fewer. Many parents *think* there are more because sensational stories of child kidnappings get constant coverage in the media.

Most crimes against kids are committed by people they know, not by strangers. So instead of warning them about stranger danger, teach them the three R's: *Recognize* that no one is allowed to touch you where your bathing suit covers. *Resist* by yelling, kicking, or running away. Don't be nice if someone is bothering you. *Report* what happened. Even if the person makes you promise not to tell . . . *tell.* Reassure your kids that you will not be mad at them no matter what happened.

2. **"But what if something happens?"** Verbalized or not, many parents believe that "If I watch my kid every second nothing bad will happen." First, that's not true. Second, you can't possibly watch your kid every second. Third, if you keep that tight a hold on your children, they will never learn to be independent. Just because something *might* happen is not a reason to keep kids locked up inside forever. As Let Grow founder Lenore Skenazy says, "thinking that one crime anywhere means no one is safe anywhere, ever" is "a cult of innumeracy." Parents don't think "What if something happens?" every time they get in a car with their kid, and many, many more kids die in car accidents than from kidnappings. Warwick Cairns, author of the book *How to*

Live Dangerously, calculates that if for some bizarre reason you *wanted* your kid to get kidnapped, they would have to be outside unattended for 750,000 years on average for that to happen.

3. **"Are you sure that's safe?"** Letting kids roam in their neighborhoods is not actually all that risky. To quote Skenazy again, "A lot of parents today are really bad at assessing risk. They see no difference between letting their children walk to school and letting them walk through a firing range. When they picture their kids riding their bikes to a birthday party, they see them dodging Mack trucks with brake problems. To let their children play unsupervised in a park at age 8 or 10 or even 13 seems about as responsible as throwing them in the shark tank at Sea World with their pockets full of meatballs." In reality, letting kids walk or bike to school, for example, is very safe. We're not talking about crazy risks here—your kids should still be wearing bike helmets and looking both ways. But if you never let your child do anything that might possibly be a little risky, they'll never learn how to live in the world.

4. **"Could I get arrested?"** Most states do not specify how old a child needs to be before they can be left at home alone. Some states, including Utah, Oklahoma, Virginia, Connecticut, Colorado, Illinois, Montana, and Texas have passed "Reasonable Childhood Independence" laws explicitly saying it is not illegal for children to play outside or walk to school alone. It's worth looking into the laws in your state. In the last few years, there's been more and

more pushback against shaming parents who let kids have freedom—the tide is turning.

5. **"But I have too much homework to cook dinner/do my own laundry."** This is occasionally true, but very rarely. Most kids spend much more time with screen entertainment than they do on homework. Even if your kid does have a lot of homework or activities, it's usually more of a planning issue. One work-around is for your kid's dinner-cooking night to be Friday, Saturday, or Sunday, when they are less likely to have homework or activities. Laundry can be done on weekends, on days off from school, and so on. And more household chores doesn't mean worse academic performance—quite the opposite. In a large study of elementary school kids, those who did chores scored higher on a standardized test in math. They also felt more competent.

6. **"But none of my friends do that!"** Consider teaming up with other parents to ask your kids' school to do the "Let Grow Experience," a homework assignment that asks kids in grades K–8 to "go home and do something new on your own with your parents' permission but without your parents: Walk the dog, make a meal, run an errand." The assignment can be weekly, monthly, twice a year—whatever the school wants—and takes about 15 minutes of class time. Having other parents letting go at the same time makes it less guilt-inducing—and then your kid isn't the "only one" doing it. There's also a high school version called the "Independence Inventory" where teens can check off activities

like the ones in this chapter. Another idea to suggest to elementary schools: a Let Grow Play Club where schools stay open after release time for kids to play together, with adults supervising but intervening only in emergencies. It's like a wildlife preserve for face-to-face socializing and fun—what childhood used to be like.

7. **"But Mom/Dad, I'm scared to do that."** Good! Then do it and you won't be scared of it anymore!

RULE 9: BEWARE THE LAPTOP— AND THE GAMING CONSOLE, AND THE TABLET, AND . . .

"What are you up to?" I asked our 6th grader, J, who was ensconced under a comforter on the top bunk. "Doing my iReady," she said, referring to the math and reading program used in our school district. But was she really? I have no idea. She was using a laptop issued by her school, and it had YouTube on it. I had no way of knowing if she was really doing her homework unless I hovered over her the whole time, which wasn't practical.

Being a parent today often means playing Whack-A-Mole with devices. Just as you have one under control, another pops up.

Out of all the areas covered in this book, I made the most parental errors in this category, especially with my kids and their laptops. So I'm going to tell you what I wish I had known earlier. That way, with any luck, you won't make the same mistakes.

If you follow the 8 rules we've covered so far, you'll be way ahead of the game with your kids. They won't have the internet in their pocket at 10. They won't be sitting across from you at a restaurant at age 14 unable to tear their eyes from TikTok. They won't be staying up until 2 a.m. on their phones. But they very well might be overly attached to their iPad, addicted to gaming, or doing things they shouldn't be doing on their laptops.

There are four non-phone devices that pop up the most often: tablets, gaming consoles, school laptops, and personal laptops.

THE TABLET

It's very common for younger kids and even toddlers to have their own iPad, Amazon Fire, or Samsung Galaxy tablet. I once saw a young boy with a tablet hung around his neck. Gen Z's name for Gen Alpha, the kids just younger than them, is "crusty iPad kids." Not only are they usually holding an iPad, but apparently they don't wash their hands before they use it, which is how it becomes crusty.

Do not give your kids their own tablets. As much as possible, kids should be watching their shows on a regular TV instead of on a tablet. That way it's much easier to keep track of what they're watching and how long they've been watching it. Yes, I know kids' shows are annoying to listen to (I know this because iPads didn't exist when my oldest was a toddler). But if kids have their own personal device, they're going to watch videos a lot more. And remember, tablets can do everything phones can do, including social media.

What about during travel? Tablets have certainly made flying with young children much easier. One solution is to let them use your tablet or your spouse's tablet on the plane—they're likely sitting next to you or close, so you'll be able to see what they are doing. Planes are one place where it probably makes some sense for kids to have screen time.

Long car rides are more of a judgment call for device time. Unlike on a plane, rowdy kids aren't going to disturb other passengers, and there's more to see out the window and more opportunities to get out of the vehicle and take a break if necessary. If a movie or two will help keep the peace, put it on the car's entertainment system if you have one—then you'll know exactly what they are watching and there's a natural end point. Or siblings can watch together on a single tablet. When our kids were young, we'd often say they could watch one movie or two TV episodes during a car ride and that was it. As a result, there was at least some looking out the window, conversation, and playing games. When each kid has their own device, it's a lot harder to limit what they're doing.

In sum, the rule is: Don't give kids their own tablet. If there's a situation where it might come in handy, they can borrow yours.

THE GAMING CONSOLE

The most important rule is this: Never put a gaming console or desktop computer in your kid's bedroom. That makes it way too easy for them to game into the wee hours or never finish their homework even if they've been in their bedroom the whole evening.

Gaming is the favorite activity of many kids, especially boys. As Jonathan Haidt documents in *The Anxious Generation*, boys have increasingly pulled away from physical activities like outside play and have instead invested their time and energy in the virtual world. Gaming is also popular with many girls, especially *Minecraft* and *Roblox*.

Gaming is the primary way some kids spend time with their friends. Since gaming is in real time and done in small groups, it's not as obviously toxic as social media. If your kid has a friend they game with, try to get them together in person. Even if they end up gaming side by side, at least they'll have some social interaction apart from the game. Games played alone, especially on phones, are less likely to have benefits as they don't involve social interaction.

Games are designed to be extremely engaging. It's difficult for many kids to stop playing and do homework or come to dinner. One young man told me he had to give up gaming entirely when he went to college because if he kept it up he'd never do anything else. In the Q&A after my talks, parents frequently ask me how to get their sons to stop spending all of their time gaming. Many kids have an unhealthy relationship with gaming.

To keep kids' gaming from becoming unhealthy, use parental controls. You'll want to do this on every device they use to game. Gaming consoles like the Sony PlayStation and Nintendo Switch have built-in parental controls. You can use the operating system parental controls or third-party software for laptops and phones.

What parental controls should you install to limit gaming? The list is similar to the parental controls covered in Rule 6:

1. **Shut down the device or app after your kid's bedtime** (or, ideally, start a half hour before bedtime so they have time to wind down before sleep).

2. **No downloading apps** (so you'll know what games they are playing). Yes, they might play games on their friends' devices, but at least you'll know what they're doing at home on their laptops or phones.

3. **Time limits.** Since kids often play different games across different devices, make sure you're thinking of time limits as *total* gaming time, including phone games, console games, and computer games. An hour a day is a reasonable limit for gaming time on weekdays (Monday through Thursday), and two hours on weekend days (Friday evening, Saturday, and Sunday). Some families say no gaming on weekdays, only on weekends, which can also be a good strategy (though you'll still want a daily limit on the weekends, maybe two or three hours tops).

   Another approach is to allow kids to game after they've finished their household jobs and homework for the day. But some kids will say they've finished their homework when they haven't or will rush through their homework to get to gaming. And what about studying for tests? Kids can easily say they've studied "enough," and how can you know? That's why it's necessary to set time limits or not allow gaming on school nights at all.

No matter what limits you set, make sure your kid spends time doing things other than gaming, like sports, hobbies, getting outside, or reading. If gaming is the only thing they're interested in, things have to change. As Figure 9.1 shows, heavy gamers are nearly twice as likely to be depressed as lighter users. Among boys, there's no link to depression with 1 or 2 hours a day of gaming, but after that the risk of depression increases steadily.

One other caveat: Be aware of what games your kids are playing. Some games are extremely violent and/or (to put it mildly) don't teach the values you want your kids to have (ahem, *Grand Theft Auto*). Many kids play *Minecraft*, which is rated for kids 10 and up. Make sure they are playing using a child account since that has built-in protections. In many online games, unknown adults can talk with children unless that ability has been turned off.

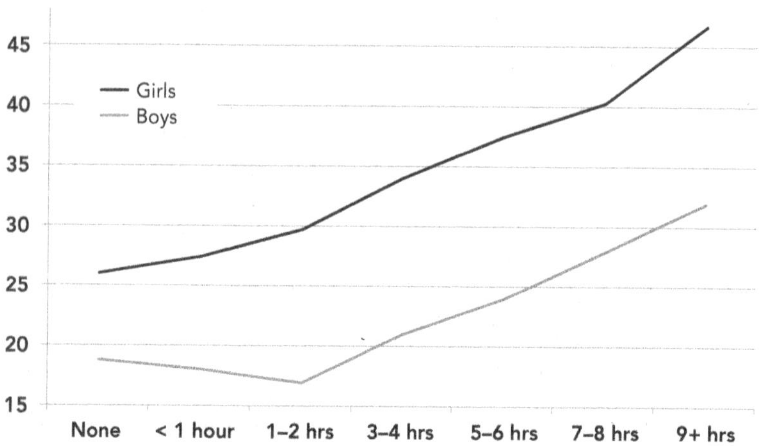

Figure 9.1: Hours per day gaming and percent depressed, U.S. 8th and 10th graders

Source: Monitoring the Future survey, 2018–2023

Note: Controlled for race/ethnicity, mother's education level, and grade. Depressive symptoms are measured by six items, and teens are considered depressed if their average score is a 3 or above on a 5-point scale.

And whatever game your kid is playing, ensure they can't make in-app purchases. One mom I know opened her credit card statement to find that her 10-year-old son had charged thousands of dollars in a game he was playing, not realizing he was spending real money.

In sum, the rules for gaming are:

- No gaming consoles or desktop computers in kids' bedrooms.
- Use parental controls to make sure they're not gaming after bedtime and aren't downloading games you don't know about.
- Set time limits for gaming, especially on school nights.

THE SCHOOL LAPTOP

Most schools have bought in wholesale to the idea of a 1:1 student-device ratio, especially once kids get to middle school. It's true that educational software can be useful, and being able to access homework assignments online is extremely convenient. But the school laptop has been the bane of my existence. You can't put parental controls on it, and it often comes preloaded with apps that are occasionally educational but always distracting, like YouTube. The absence of parental controls also means you can't have the laptop shut down at bedtime or restrict how much time your kid spends watching videos.

The good news is school laptops do block most inappropriate websites, including social media and pornography sites. Sometimes that software makes odd mistakes, though—for example, J couldn't use her school laptop to look up how to pronounce words because the device blocked any search that started with "pron"—likely because that's a typo for "porn." And even with that, the filters apparently don't work very well—a Common Sense Media survey found that about 11% of teens had viewed pornography *on a school-issued device during the school day*. The number who did so at home is presumably much higher.

School iPads can be just as bad or worse, since kids (and adults) associate them with entertainment. At one middle school I visited, a 7th-grade teacher said a parent once called to complain that she'd been assigning too much homework on the iPad that semester. "I haven't assigned *any* homework on the iPad yet this semester," the teacher told the parent. We all know what had happened: The kid was watching videos on the school iPad and telling his mother he was doing homework.

There are a few ways forward. One is to put the school laptop aside and buy your child their own laptop, if you can afford it. That way you can put parental controls on it (more on this below). Another solution is to talk to the school administration about what they allow on school devices. For example, you can ask if access to YouTube is truly necessary. It's tough, though, because many teachers ask students to watch videos for homework assignments. But perhaps the video can be accessed as a stand-alone rather than through YouTube, whose algorithm is designed to keep kids watching long after the video required for class is over. Or suggest that teachers give homework on paper instead of online. Paper is a lot less distracting for kids and a lot easier for parents to monitor.

I worded this rule as "beware" for a reason: There is not an easy solution here, but it helps to at least be aware that school laptops are not as locked down as they should be. If your kid has been doing homework for three hours straight, casually ask if you can help—and take a look at the screen or the browser history. Then you might need to talk about how easy it is to get distracted by videos, especially if you're struggling with doing something difficult. Most adults have had that experience, too, and you can say so. We all have to remember that tech companies have designed their apps to distract us, and that goes for apps on school laptops, too.

THE PERSONAL LAPTOP

Once kids get to middle school, teachers start requiring a lot more homework done using a computer. It quickly becomes impractical for a kid to share a computer with other members of the family. This is when the laptop monster runs out from under the bed and steals your children.

If your kids' school doesn't provide laptops or if you (or your kids) are frustrated with the school laptop, it's time to get your kid their own personal laptop. True confessions: This is where I screwed up. Maybe because most social media apps are designed for phones, maybe because I was used to the school laptop, maybe because I put my husband in charge of the purchase, or maybe because I trusted E because we'd talked at length about the downsides of social media, E—14 at the time—ended up with a personal laptop without any websites blocked. A few months later, I found out she had opened Tik-

Tok and Instagram accounts on it. Then we had to backtrack and block social media sites.

Avoid my mistake and use parental controls to block social media and inappropriate sites *before* you give your kid a personal laptop. As I found out the hard way, nearly all social media sites can be accessed, at least in a limited way, using a laptop or other computer.

The lesson: Don't assume that your kids won't try to open social media accounts or won't access porn sites just because you talked to them about it. They probably will, because all of their friends are doing it and a teen's job is to push boundaries. Despite all of the talking we'd done about social media, and despite getting in trouble for it before, E still tried to access Instagram within three hours of getting a new laptop. This time, though, I'd installed parental control software that blocked it—and alerted me when she tried to access the site.

As with everything, delay: Don't get your kid their own laptop until you have to. In most school districts, that's going to be the beginning of middle school when teachers start posting homework online instead of sending home paper worksheets. But 11-year-olds aren't even close to ready for unfiltered internet access.

So how, exactly, do you keep kids safe if they have a personal laptop?

DEAR APPLE: I LOVE YOU, BUT YOUR PARENTAL CONTROLS SUCK

Last year, I decided I was done with J having a school laptop with no parental controls and E having a personal laptop with controls I didn't know how to use (her laptop was a Chromebook and I'm a lifelong Mac user, so I relied on my PC-using husband to administer the controls). I found a good sale on two lower-end Mac laptops, figuring they'd make nice Christmas gifts.

That's when the ordeal began. Once again, I'll let you in on my mistakes so you don't make the same ones.

The first issue came in the first few minutes of setting up the laptop—I didn't know whether to use my Apple account or get one for my kid. I figured it was going to be her computer, so I got an account for her and used it in the setup process. I then found out there was no way to designate the original account as a child's; that account automatically had administrator privileges, meaning she could change everything I did to try to make the laptop safe for her. So I had to erase the computer back to factory settings and start over. Thus: Use your account to set up the computer first and *then* create a "standard" (non-administrator) account for your kid. (Note to Apple: Please have a button in the setup process to designate that the device is for a child. That would make the setup process, and everything else, much easier.)

After I got E's account set up, I thought it would be smooth sailing. I was wrong. Trying to set up the Apple parental controls was an hours-long exercise in frustration. When I looked online for how to set up parental controls on an Apple device, it told me the best way was to sign up for Family Sharing. But to do that, E would need to respond to an email. She was at school, plus I shouldn't need my kid's permission to add parental controls. So that was out. The top of the webpage for setting up Screen Time for a child said you didn't need Family

Sharing, but then the instructions said you *did* need Family Sharing. If the laptop wasn't so pretty (not to mention expensive), I might have thrown it.

I did spot a place in the Screen Time section (under Settings) where I could toggle on "Use a passcode to secure Screen Time settings." Yay, another password to remember! However, that did allow me to toggle on appealing settings like "Communication Safety" (which blocks nude pictures) and set Downtime so the laptop wouldn't work overnight.

I then went into App Limits to try to block certain websites, but after I entered them I realized the Save button was grayed out. What? I eventually realized you had to put in a time limit of at least a minute to save it—App Limits is only for time limits, not for outright blocking of websites. I finally found the website blocks under Content & Privacy, and then the section called App Store, Media, Web, and Games, and then a button with "Customize" where, at long last, I typed in the URLs for Pornhub, TikTok, Instagram, and Discord.

At this point I severely needed a nap.

Instead, I figured I would try some third-party parental control software with the hope it might be easier to use. I paid $99.50 a year for a "complete" subscription to Qustodio, which I'd heard works well with Mac laptops. There's also a $54.95-a-year "basic" option with many of the same features.

This was new password number four for the day, but boy, was it worth it. I downloaded the software onto E's laptop and then logged back into my account on my computer. Within a few seconds, I was able to set the laptop to shut down between 9:30 p.m. and 7:00 a.m. Under web filtering, whole categories of websites were already blocked, including those dedicated to gambling, violence, or pornography. This is much better than trying to block specific websites with the device controls, since how are parents supposed to know the URLs of all of the inappropriate sites? There are hundreds, and they keep changing. I also blocked the social networks category (their name for social media). It's also possible to add specific websites to block or to allow. This is all under a menu called "Rules."

There's also a Dashboard where you can do other things like set a total time limit for the device and a Timeline where you can see what your kids have been doing. The best part: After I installed the software, I could see and control everything from my own computer without having to get into E's laptop. No one wants to wrestle a laptop out of a teen's hands.

The only thing I couldn't figure out how to do in Qustodio was to set time limits for certain websites (I'm looking at you, YouTube). It also wasn't clear which websites were in each category—like entertainment, for example, which blocked things like Netflix, which I expected, but also blocked the Taylor Swift merch website. Fortunately it was very easy to add specific websites back in. Overall, the third-party software was much easier to set up than the controls included with the laptop's operating system.

Now I just have to set up J's laptop. Maybe after that nap.

LAPTOP PARENTAL CONTROLS: THE SUMMARY

- **If you have more time and patience than money:** Rely on the device controls, which are free but harder to use. On a Mac, follow the steps below (similar controls are available on Chromebooks using Google Family Link).

1. If you're setting up the laptop for the first time, use your Apple account, not your child's. That way the administrator account will be yours.
2. Set up a "standard" (not administrator) account for your child.
3. In the Apple menu on your child's laptop, go to Settings, then Screen Time.
4. Toggle on "Use a passcode to secure Screen Time settings."
5. Toggle on "Communication Safety."
6. Set a bedtime schedule for Downtime.
7. Go to Content & Privacy, and then App Store, Media, Web, and Games, then "Customize" to block porn and social media sites.
8. Go to App Limits to set a time limit for certain websites—for example, you might set a daily time limit of an hour a day for YouTube.com.

- **If you have a little money and less time and patience:** Set up the laptop and then install third-party parental control software.

1. If you're setting up the laptop for the first time, use your account and information, not your child's.
2. Set up a "standard" (not administrator) account for your child.

3. On your computer or phone, purchase a subscription to third-party control software such as Qustodio, Net Nanny, or Bark.

4. On your child's laptop, download the software and install it.

5. Back on your computer or phone, set the limits you want for your child's laptop.

6. If the software doesn't include the ability to set a time limit on certain websites, see step 8 above to do that on a Mac. On Android devices and Chromebooks, you can use Family Link, tap Controls, and then App Limits.

I suggest setting up the most important rules in *both* the device controls and in the third-party software. I get a daily email from Qustodio about my kids' time on their laptops, and one day I noticed E had spent more time than her usual limit. When I went to the account, I discovered many of the controls had been reset. Her bedtime (when the laptop shuts off) was set at 11:45 p.m. instead of 9:30 p.m. and Instagram was no longer blocked. I eventually found out that she had snuck into my home office, pulled up the Qustodio website, and changed the control settings (!). When I confronted her about it, she said, "But most of what I did didn't even work!" (the world's lamest excuse). That's because I'd also set her bedtime and blocked Instagram in the device controls (see the "If you have more time and patience than money" instructions earlier). Although I was slightly proud I'd somehow technologically outsmarted a teenager, I also felt dumb that I hadn't password-protected my desktop computer. I do now.

Also realize you may have to block some websites specifically. For example, Qustodio doesn't include Snapchat under "social networks"—no idea why. I'd blocked that category for E and J, but then one day the telltale yellow-and-black ghost icon appeared on the kids' Qustodio activities dashboard. On the blocked list it went.

HOW MUCH TIME SHOULD MY KIDS BE SPENDING ON SCREENS OVERALL?

I get this question at talks all the time, and never know exactly what to say. Some kids learn how to play piano using a tablet. Some love making videos. Some watch YouTube videos to learn how to do their math homework. Devices are clearly not all bad, just as they're not all good.

Again, everything in moderation is an excellent rule. With the average American teen spending five hours a day on social media, though, many kids are clearly way beyond moderate screen use. It's clear parents need to step in with rules like those in this book. But it's also good to be aware of the creative and expressive ways kids can use devices.

Time limits make sense for specific activities, like social media and gaming. But with kids using their laptops for homework, taking pictures with their phones, and using technology in many other ways, it's difficult to settle on a total time limit. One good rule of thumb: Screen time for entertainment (which definitely includes social media and gaming) shouldn't interfere with other activities that are essential for kids' development, like sleeping, studying, exercising, and interacting with other people face-to-face.

When I first gave E and J their new laptops, I put a total time limit of four hours a day on them, thinking about everything they used them for. I later realized I'd need to vary the limit by the day. On school days the limit might need to be more like five or six hours if they were taking their laptops to school and using them there. But for weekends and breaks, I settled on a limit of two hours a day, so then they would get off the laptop and go do other things. Fortunately the Qustodio software made changing the time limit easy, even on the fly.

COMMON OBSTACLES AND PUSHBACKS

1. **"But, Mom/Dad, I'm doing my homework—I need more time!"** This usually means they are watching YouTube (or were, and are just now scrambling to get their homework done). It's impossible to tell if they are actually doing their homework, which is one of the main reasons to use parental controls. It makes sense to give an occasional extension for homework. But if it's every night, you should probably have a discussion about time management with your kid. If you use third-party software, you might also be able to see if they have been gaming or on YouTube when they said they were doing their homework.

2. **"I promise I won't [go on social media, watch YouTube for more than an hour, search for porn.]"** When I've made mistakes with my kids around tech, it's (sadly) been because I trusted them too much. Unfortunately, kids' promises

mean little against social pressure, engaging games, and social media algorithms. Instead of having them promise they won't spend more than an hour on YouTube, set that limit in parental controls. Block social media websites if you don't want them on social media. The same goes for porn sites.

3. **"Kids will find a way no matter what you do."** Right, that's why we should stop enforcing alcohol laws, because kids are going to drink anyway. No one would argue this, because a lot fewer teens use alcohol than if we didn't enforce the laws. Similarly: Yes, some kids will use their friend's laptop to look at Instagram—but if they can't access it from their own device, they will use it a lot less often. It's true some kids find ways around parental controls, but most don't, and even when they do there's usually another solution—physically taking devices overnight, for example, or installing third-party parental control software. This is yet another time when you can come back to the mantra "Don't let the perfect be the enemy of the good." Do what you can, do your best, and your kids will benefit even if a few things break through the safety net.

RULE 10:
ADVOCATE FOR NO PHONES DURING THE SCHOOL DAY

The stories are everywhere.

Mitchell Rutherford taught biology at a public high school in Arizona for 11 years. Students' phones were not supposed to be out during class, but it was up to teachers to enforce that policy. A few years ago, students would put their phones away when he asked, Rutherford says. "Now, you can ask them, bug them, remind them, and try to punish them, and still nothing works," he said. He quit his teaching job.

Minneapolis middle school science teacher Laura Kimball taught in a school with a similar policy. "Every day is a constant struggle against cellphone usage," she said. She, too, quit her job.

If you Google "teacher quit because of phones," you'll find story after story of teachers who could no longer deal with the constant battles over phones in the classroom. Seventy-two percent of high school teachers say that students being distracted by their phones in the classroom is a major problem.

It doesn't have to be this way. One simple rule can solve it: No phones during the school day, bell to bell. That works better than more piecemeal policies because it's straightforward and covers all classrooms and the whole school day. A bell-to-bell rule accomplishes several important goals. For example:

1. **More focus in the classroom.** Phones are a huge distraction from classroom learning. If school policy says phones are fine everywhere but classrooms, teachers have to spend class time chasing students off phones or decide to not enforce the rule. And when phones are accessible in the classroom, academic performance suffers. Several studies have found that the mere presence of a smartphone reduces cognitive performance.

2. **More face-to-face socializing at lunch.** When students can access their phones during lunch, lunchrooms are eerily quiet as students use their phones instead of talking to each other.

3. **Learning how to live without the constant presence of a phone.** With a bell-to-bell policy, kids have the experience of being away from their phones for at least six hours a day.

4. **Less fighting and drama.** No phones means no bullying via text, no taking videos, and no social media drama during the school day. In a rural district in Colorado, more than half of the school's disciplinary issues were due to phones, including incidents of cyberbullying, recording fights, and videoing students in bathrooms without their permission.

> When the North Adams school district in Massachusetts banned phones during the school day, discipline referrals dropped a stunning 75%.

School phone policies work best if students are required to physically put their phones in a central location in the school building or if the school provides devices (like those made by the company Yondr) that lock phones in a pouch for the day. After a New York public school introduced Yondr pouches, administrators reported "increased student engagement in the classroom, less time spent in the bathrooms and hallways, more genuine connections within the community, and a decrease in reports of cyberbullying." A Connecticut high school reported a 35% decline in suspensions and a 50% drop in students getting sent to the principal's office after Yondr pouches were introduced.

Second best is a rule that phones need to be kept in lockers or backpacks, but that's harder to enforce. It's still better than a looser policy, though. "We had one year with a strict cellphone policy of 'if we see it, it's confiscated.' This worked!" said Kimball, the former middle school teacher. "The number of fights dramatically decreased; students were on time to class and more focused once there."

The physical accessibility of the phone matters the most. When students can access their phones, many will take them out even if there's a "no phones in the classroom" policy. That's partially because many teachers have, somewhat understandably, given up trying to fight kids over their phones. "If the policy isn't clear and consistent at school, you get a slippery slope," says Missouri science teacher Noelle Gilzow. "You have the 'cool' teacher who lets me use my cellphone in class. And then there is the 'mean' teacher who does not. . . . it sets up a bad dynamic, an unhealthy culture in the building."

My children's school district has a policy disallowing phone use during instructional time, but students are not required to keep their phones in any particular place. As a result, it's a free-for-all, and phone use—even during class—is rampant. Many teachers allow students to use their phones once they have finished their work, which makes me wonder how many students are rushing through their work to be able to use their phones. Even when teachers require students to put their phones away, some students will go to the bathroom and use their phones there. "From the classrooms you can hear people in the bathroom laughing at TikToks," J told me when she was in 7th grade.

K told me students routinely used their phones during class in high school. She once sat behind a boy who was watching pornography in the middle of class. Her experience is apparently not rare: In a Common Sense Media survey, one out of four teens said they watched adult content during the school day. Half of those said they used a school-issued device to do so.

"In the early 1960s, when my parents were in high school, they received free sampler packs of cigarettes on their cafeteria trays," writes Russell Shaw, the head of school at Georgetown Day School in Washington, DC. "I believe that future generations will look back with the same incredulity at our acceptance of phones in schools." Another way to think about it: Back in the 1980s, would schools have allowed students to bring their own TVs to school? Of course not, but allowing phones—which are even more powerful entertainment devices than TVs—is just as bad or worse. "We're competing with Netflix, FaceTime, texting," says science teacher Gilzow. "They're even watching March Madness!"

A study of Norwegian middle schools found that smartphone bans led to improved academic performance, less bullying, and better mental health, especially for girls. The vast majority of American teachers—83%—support prohibiting student phone use during the entire school day. "I don't want to be the phone police. I want to teach," said California high school art teacher Devon Espejo.

THE ACADEMIC CONSEQUENCES

Loose phone policies at schools have been a disaster for learning. The international PISA study, which gives 15-year-olds standardized tests in math, reading, and science, is the gold standard for assessing the academic performance of teens around the world. PISA test scores have been declining since the early 2010s, around the time smartphones became popular (for example, Figure 10.1 on the following page shows scores for Western Europe). For most teens, what school subject can possibly compete with the portal to fun and friends in the palm of their hand?

One especially sad example is Finland, once known for having the best school system in the world. In 2022, teens in Finland admitted to using their devices during the school day for non-school purposes for nearly ninety minutes. Perhaps as a result, the test scores of Finnish students plummeted between 2012 and 2022. In countries such as Japan,

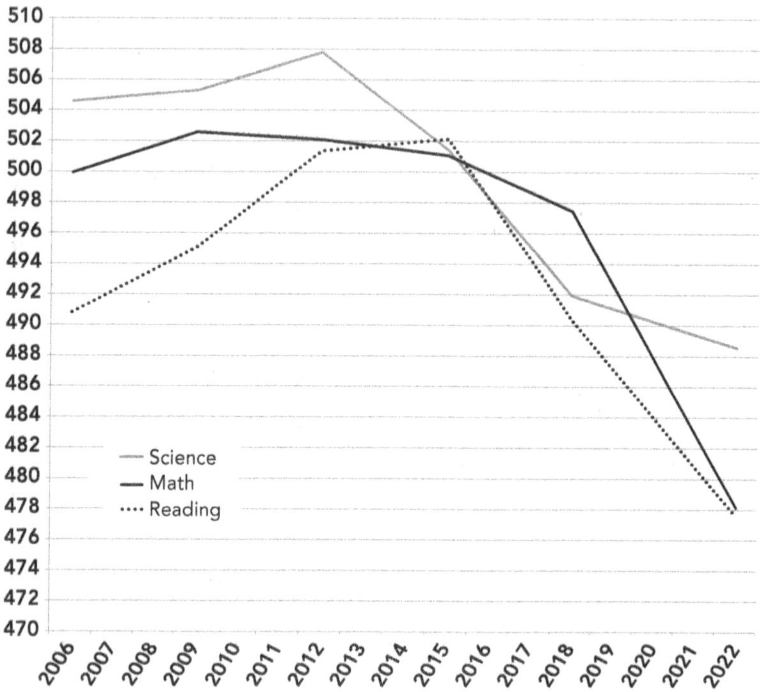

Figure 10.1: Scores on standardized tests measuring academic performance in math, reading, and science, 15-year-olds in Western European countries, 2006–2022

Source: Programme for International Student Assessment (PISA), administered by OCED

Note: The region average is weighted by the population size of each country. Data are from Austria, Belgium, Denmark, Finland, France, Germany, Italy, the Netherlands, Norway, Portugal, Spain, Sweden, and Switzerland.

where students spend less than half an hour on their phones for leisure during the school day, academic performance has instead stayed steady.

Test scores in math and reading have also declined among middle school students. In the National Assessment of Educational Progress—known as the Nation's Report Card—U.S. 8th graders' academic performance began to decline after

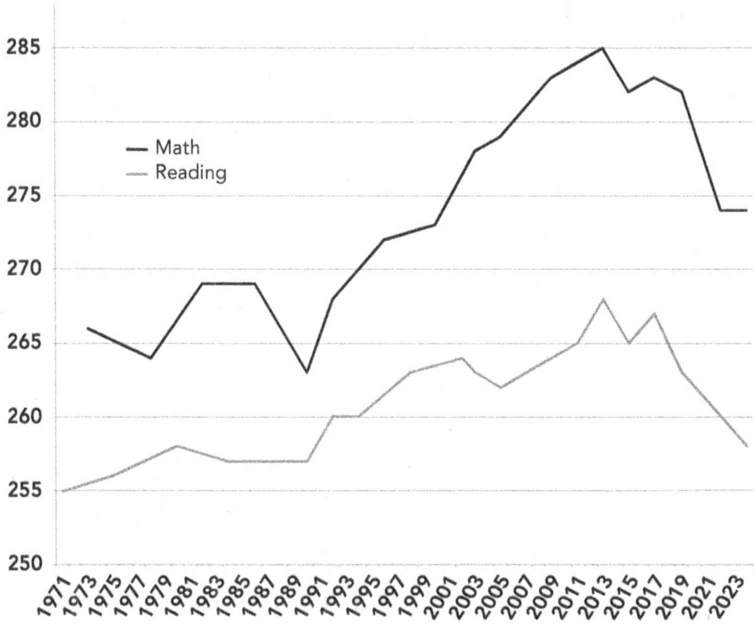

Figure 10.2: Math and reading test scores, U.S. 8th graders, 1971–2024

Source: National Assessment of Educational Progress

2012. That was after decades of improving performance (see Figure 10.2 above).

Trend studies like this can't show that lax phone policies directly lead to worse performance, but experimental studies can. The results are consistent: Students with access to devices during class perform more poorly on tests, primarily because phones are so distracting. In one experiment, college students were randomly assigned to either hand their phone in or keep it while watching a 20-minute educational video, a format similar to college lectures. They then took a quiz on what they saw. Students who didn't have their phones scored seven percentage points higher on the test than those who kept their phones. A follow-up study found an even bigger difference—those without access to their phones scored 13 percentage points higher on the test. Thus, removing phones from the classroom can make a difference between an A and a B, or failing a class versus passing it.

THE SOCIAL CONSEQUENCES

The consequences of phones in school aren't just academic. Access to phones during lunch and non-classroom time often means students aren't talking to each other. Shaw, the Georgetown Day School head, describes watching the students at his school looking at their screens instead of fully engaging with one another. "I've watched students who struggle to make friends not learn how to, because they can retreat into the short-term safety of their phones rather than tolerate the discomfort that often precedes finding one's way into a conversation," he writes. "Phones teach our students to abandon the eyes of the person they're speaking to in order to glance at a newly arrived text or Snapchat message."

Many Gen Zers feel that discomfort well into young adulthood. College students frequently tell me they prefer texting because they can think over their response. Many are socially anxious and say they don't feel safe talking to other people face-to-face, which they often describe using the phrase "emotional safety." "I believe nobody can guarantee emotional safety," a 19-year-old wrote. "You can always take precautions for someone hurting you physically, but you cannot really help but listen when someone is talking to you."

When I give presentations on generations in the workplace,

managers frequently tell me that Gen Z's deficient social skills are a big problem. "They don't have the soft skills required for the jobs we're hiring for," one said. If students don't have their phones at lunch, they will have more opportunities to develop these skills.

A bell-to-bell ban on phones would also help teens who don't want to be on their phones at lunch or during breaks, but feel they have to be because their friends are looking at their screens. After I gave a presentation at a high school in Texas, a sophomore boy told me he really wanted to connect with his friends at lunch, but most of them wanted to play games on their phones instead. He asked me what he could do to change that. My heart broke a little, because the truth is there's not much he can do. But if his school banned phones during lunch, the problem would immediately go away.

WHAT CAN PARENTS DO?

Of course, the phone policy at your child's school is not directly under your control—unless private school is an option and you choose a school partially based on their phone policy, which some parents do. But for most of us, it's not something we can directly change.

Still, we can try. If your kid's school has anything other than a bell-to-bell ban, it's time to spring into action. But where to start?

I had this same question myself since I wanted to send an email to my kids' high school principal about this issue. But when I went looking for an email template for contacting school administrators about phone bans, I couldn't find anything useful.

Eventually I got in touch with Delaney Ruston, MD, who produced *Screenagers*, one of the first documentaries about teens and tech. She now heads a program called Away for the Day that advocates for bell-to-bell phone bans at schools. Dr. Ruston drafted an email template parents can send to school principals and district superintendents. Here it is with a few edits and additions from me:

Dear [Administrator's Name],

I am a parent of a [your child's grade] grader at [School's Name]. I am hoping you will consider implementing a "no phones during the school day" policy that bans students from using their cellphones or smartwatches from the beginning to the end of the school day.

Separating students from their devices during school hours allows them an opportunity to focus on learning, socializing, and interacting face-to-face with peers, friends, and school staff instead of being distracted by the constant pull of their devices. The benefits of keeping phones off and away all day at school will be immense.

Here are just a few reasons why putting a phone ban in place is imperative:

- **Phone use during school hours is rampant.** Ninety-seven percent of students aged 11 to 17 used their phones during the school day for an average of 46 minutes, according to Common Sense Media. More recent data shows students using their phones an average of 90 minutes during the school day.
- **Academic performance is suffering.** Students can take up to 20 minutes to refocus on their lesson after being

distracted, resulting in poorer academic achievement. Standardized test scores are down around the world, and those declines began in the early 2010s as smartphones became popular.

- **Phones are often the root cause of discipline issues.** When a Massachusetts school district banned phone use during the school day, discipline referrals dropped by 75%.
- **Teachers are tired of fighting for students' attention.** Ninety percent of teachers support banning cellphone use during instructional hours, and 83% favor cellphone bans for the entire school day, according to a 2024 National Education Association (NEA) poll.
- **Social skills are atrophying.** When students have access to their phones during passing periods and lunch, they are staring at screens instead of interacting face-to-face with their peers and developing crucial social skills.

I realize that instituting a ban and finding places for phones to be locked away is challenging.

Here's one source that might help: The Away for the Day campaign from the makers of the Screenagers documentaries offers support for instituting a smartphone ban in schools and links to scientific data, testimonials, and example policies in effect at schools across the country.

Please let me know how I can help get an Away for the Day cellphone policy at our school from bell to bell.

Thank you so much.

Sincerely,
[Your name]

Feel free to modify this to add issues you think are important or tweak it for the situation at your child's school. It's a place to start. If you can, talk to other parents who are also concerned about the impact of phones in schools. If the principal or superintendent hears from many parents, the policy is more likely to change.

Even if your kids' school allows phones and won't change their policy, you can still choose to not text or call your children during school hours. It's very tempting to text them with that question you forgot to ask them before school, but it can almost always wait. Teachers tell me students feel anxious when their parents text them during the day, especially about their grades. Think about it this way: When you were in high school, would you have wanted your parents to be able to constantly contact you during the school day? I'm guessing not.

ALSO: ADVOCATE FOR LOW-TECH SCHOOLS

A decade ago, many schools trumpeted their 1:1 device ratio—every kid gets an iPad or laptop! This will be great for learning!

It wasn't, and the research is pretty clear on why. Several studies have found that reading on paper leads to significantly better reading comprehension than reading digitally. U.S. 4th and 8th graders who spent more time using digital devices in language arts classes performed worse on reading tests. College students who took handwritten notes were 58% more likely to get A's in college courses than those who typed notes on laptops, and those who typed notes were 75% more likely to fail the course than those who handwrote notes. Many of these studies are experimental, meaning they show a direct line of causation between paper versus digital note-taking and academic performance.

Digital homework can also cause issues. One study observed middle school, high school, and college students studying in their homes. Students lasted an average of six minutes studying on their laptops before they started browsing social media or texting. Even with someone observing them, students spent a third of their "study" time not studying.

The amount of tech used at school and for homework is another area where parents don't have direct control. But they can talk to their kids' teachers and explain how distracted their kids are when they have homework on their laptops or tablets. Could more homework be assigned on paper, perhaps? If they have the option of private school, parents can also vote with their feet, choosing schools with less emphasis on devices. Waldorf schools, which avoid all screens until at least 7th grade, are (ironically—or not) very popular in Silicon Valley, the home of many tech companies.

What about the idea that students need to use devices to develop 21st-century skills? The problem is technology is constantly changing. As Everyschool founder Amy Tyson points out, a child starting school in this decade won't retire until the 2080s. We can't predict how digital tools will change. But we can predict that our kids will need good attention spans and soft skills, and devices undermine both.

COMMON OBSTACLES AND PUSHBACKS

School principals routinely tell me that they get the most resistance to a phone ban not from students but from parents.

Because most parents didn't grow up with smartphones, I suspect many aren't aware of how negatively phones impact academic performance. Most parents come on board with phone bans when they hear about the research.

Still, academic performance isn't the only consideration. If you're interested in getting a bell-to-bell phone ban instituted at your child's school, it can help to know how to counter some of the arguments you might hear from your fellow parents. These are also things you might be wondering about yourself.

1. **"I want to be able to contact my child during school hours."** You can: Call the front desk. And if it isn't important enough to call the front desk about, it can probably wait. Liz Shulman, a high school English teacher in Evanston, Illinois, says that parents "often sound very supportive of cellphone policies and want their kids to learn, but they also want access to them at all times."

   That's partially because they are trying to micromanage their kids' lives, which isn't good for them. One student in Shulman's class said his mother requires him to text her every class period. Another sent a picture of a quiz he was taking, and his mother immediately emailed the teacher to ask if he could instead take it the next day "so he can review more." When parents can continually contact students, they don't develop independence. "School is supposed to be a place where students get distance," Shulman writes. "This distinction between home and school exists to help teenagers think for themselves. Yet some students are not getting the gift of experiencing this separation."

2. **"Students need their phones in case there's a school shooting."** School safety experts agree that students having phones during a shooting is actually *more* dangerous, for at least four reasons:

   A. Students might miss important instructions during an emergency situation if they are distracted by their phones.

   B. Noise from phones may alert shooters to where people are hiding.

   C. Too many people trying to text or call at the same time from the same location can tie up bandwidth and keep authorities from communicating.

   D. Although it sounds comforting that students could contact their parents during a shooting, parents will then rush to the school, creating traffic congestion that can keep police and ambulances from getting through.

   For all of these reasons, it's actually safer if students *don't* have their phones during an active shooter situation.

3. **"My kid won't have anything to do at lunch if they don't have their phone."** I've heard this from parents, but have more often heard it from teens who say they don't have friends to sit with at lunch. That's a tough spot to be in. But if phones aren't available to anyone during lunch, students will be more likely to talk to each other and make friends. Phones block spontaneous conversation, which is

the way most friendships form. Of course, some kids have a tough time socially at school and even a phone ban won't change that. But even in this situation they don't *have* to be on their phones at lunch—they could read a book, draw, or write in a journal, for example. Learning to be without your phone, even in an awkward social situation, is a good skill.

CONCLUSION: YOU'VE GOT THIS

Those are the 10 rules. With a clear blueprint for when, why, and how your kids use electronic devices, you can feel empowered to help your family find the right balance with technology.

Still, it's easy to get frustrated. It seems like every time you think you've got a plan down, your kid finds another device, hears about another cool social media app from a friend, or comes up with yet another compelling reason they need a smartphone—right now. It's tough to follow all of the rules, and it's tough to follow them all perfectly.

But guess what? That's OK. Remember: Don't let the perfect be the enemy of the good. Do what you can. Even if you follow only half of the rules half of the time, your kid will still benefit. They got a smartphone at 13? Better than 10, and now you know to put parental controls on it. They had a TikTok account for a few months before you discovered it? At least they're not on it anymore. They were staring at their phones the whole family vacation? Take them away during the next trip.

We're not going to eliminate all technology from our kids' lives. We wouldn't want to. But we can't continue with the complete free-for-all where tech companies have stolen our kids' attention so much they're not even going out with their friends anymore. We can't pretend everything is fine when teen depression has doubled and academic performance has plummeted. We can't merely talk to our kids about limits when the social pressure, the algorithms, and their underdeveloped frontal lobes are conspiring to keep them constantly on their devices.

Parenting is so often about learning as you go. These days, with so much technology around our kids and so little regulation, our jobs are harder than ever. As I hope you saw in this book, though, you are not alone. So many of us are fighting the same battles. Not every day will be a victory, but most of them will.

Together, we can get our kids back.

ACKNOWLEDGMENTS

On a visit to New York in October 2019, I had lunch with my amazing literary agent Jill Kneerim and my fantastic editor Peter Borland. We discussed two very different book ideas: a book on all six living American generations and a book of advice for parents on managing their kids' technology use. All three of us loved both ideas, but we had to decide which one I should write first. We settled on the generations book, which—after a pause during the COVID pandemic and a long process of research—was published in April 2023, with an updated paperback edition in January 2025. *Generations* covers (at least what felt like) everything that differs across the generations, including birth rates, median incomes, age at first marriage, mental health, sexuality, political views, technology use, gender roles, self-confidence, and work attitudes.

Yet, during nearly every podcast, radio interview, TV spot, and presentation, what everyone really wanted to talk about was this: Why are kids today so depressed? And what can we do about it?

I'd known the answer to the first question since my book *iGen* was published in 2017: smartphones and social media. My answer to the second question evolved as I talked to parents around the country at speaking events and as my own three children grew up. In 2017, my children were 10, 7, and 5; today, they're 18, 15, and 13. In the end I think I wrote this book at the perfect time, when I was in the thick of raising teenagers and when parents and schools were ready to take big steps to combat the screen-based childhood.

So: Thanks to Jill and Peter for those initial conversations. To my great sadness, Jill died in 2022, but I still feel her presence, including in this book. Thank you to my agent Lucy Cleland for bringing the idea back to life and making it happen. Peter provided a cogent (and fast!) edit so we could get this book to you as quickly as possible. Hannah Frankel brought an essential Gen Z editorial perspective that I very much appreciated. One of the best things about having another book coming out is I'll get to work with the crack publicists at Atria again, including David Brown, Shida Carr, and Sierra Swanson.

My earliest readers made a huge difference with their edits and comments on selected chapters. First among those is Lenore Skenazy, the ultimate guru of kids' independence as the author of *Free-Range Kids* and the president of Let Grow. She's also a fabulously engaging writer and quite possibly the funniest person I know. Her edits on Rule 8 made the chapter much better and more comprehensive. I'm grateful to Brooke Shannon, the founder of Wait Until 8th, who provided several wonderful, practical suggestions I immediately included in the book. Anum Aslam, Jonathan Haidt, Jason Lu, Zach Rausch, and David Stein had insightful and detailed comments on several chapters and helped sharpen my thinking about social media in particular. I also drew inspiration from four authors (and fellow mothers) I admire who have written about parenting and/or technology: Michaeleen Doucleff (*Hunt, Gather, Parent*), Katherine Martinko (*Childhood Unplugged*), Clare Morell (*The Tech Exit*), and Catherine Price (*How to Break Up with Your Phone*). It's nice not to be the only one out here.

I am also extremely grateful to the parents, teachers, and students who attended my talks the last few years. I learned so much hearing about your experiences with technology and how you've tried to manage its stranglehold on our lives. Thanks to all of you for your questions and comments, which helped shape the rules in this book. I was especially motivated by the questions of middle school students, who are finding their way in a technologically saturated world and, somewhat to my surprise, are very receptive to the idea that there are better ways to live—they just want to figure out how to do it. Thanks to Dany and Claudia Elachi for sharing their story of their family's experience and making things better for Australian kids with the Heads Up Alliance.

The research described in this book could not have happened without fantastic collaborators, including Danny Blanchflower, Maartje Boer, Keith Campbell, Bell Cooper, Alina Cosma, Kevin Cummins, Spencer Deines, Mary Duffy, Eric Farley, Ellah Fessenden, Lauren Gramse, Jonathan Haidt, Jessica Hamilton, Garrett Hisler, Joanna Inchley, Helena Jericek, Thomas Joiner, Zlatan Krizan, Steinar Krokstad, Hannah Lemon, Astrid LeRoy, Julia Lima, Jimmy Lozano, Gabrielle Martin, Cooper McAllister, Zach Rausch, Lee Robertson, Megan Rogers, Elisa Ruiz, Siri Sommer, Brian Spitzberg, Gonneke Stevens, Nikhila Udupa, M'Lise Venable, Wendy Wang, and Brad Wilcox.

My thanks to all of my friends and family who were kind enough to ask about the book, including Mike and Mary Amery, Lindsey and Steve Ball, Bill Begg, Ken Bloom, Jennifer Bungo, Keith Campbell, Albert Chang, Kim and Brian Chapeau, Ellyn and L. Charap, Elizabeth Cho, Tom Daly, Amanda Davis, Jody Davis, Holly Dynoske, Jeff Green, Nick Grossman, Cyndi Haefner, Rodney Haug, Sarah and Dan Kilibarda, Dave Louden, Ron Louden, Scott Mann, Bill and Joan Moening, Brian and Roxanne Moening, Bud and Pat Moening, Kate Moening, Sarah Jane Moening, Kendel Neidermyer, Darci and Brad Olson, Sonia Orfield, Zack Orner, Trinity Perry, Greg Rumph, Adam Shah, Drew Sword, Amy and Paul Tobia, Dan Tvenge, JoAnn and Steve Twenge, Kathleen Vohs, Anna and Dusty Wetzel, Jud Wilson, Zane Zelinski, and Alice Zellmer.

Thanks to my husband Craig for running point on so many things so I have time to write. Finally, my gratitude and love to K, E, and J. K, when you said "Thank you for raising me to be an adult," I think I would have broken down in a flood of happy tears if I wasn't in an airport at the time. I am so proud of the adult you have become. J, your feedback on the cover was right on—you do indeed have an eye for these things! E and J, thanks for all the stories and being my teen ambassadors for everything from fashion to memes to slang. You're not cringe at all. You're fire. You're also sigma, though I still don't really know what that means. Love you, girls.

NOTES

INTRODUCTION

1 *When Dany Elachi's oldest daughter, Aalia, was 10*: Dany Elachi, Talk delivered at the NSW Social Media Summit, Sydney, Australia, October 2024.

1 *"I spent hours finding the perfect photos"*: K. Romalewski, "I'm a teen who used to spend hours a day scrolling. Here's how I curbed my social media habit," *Chalkbeat New York*, November 2, 2023.

2 *"Social media is built around FOMO"*: E. Vardy, "Adults and Teens Turn to 'Dumbphones' to Cut Screen Time," BBC News, June 8, 2024.

6 *Devices were interfering with kids' sleep*: G. Hisler, J. M. Twenge, and Z. Krizan, "Associations Between Screen Time and Short Sleep Duration Among Adolescents Varies by Media Type: Evidence from a Cohort Study," *Sleep Medicine* 66 (2020): 92–102.

6 *sleep deprivation is a well-established cause of depression and unhappiness*: R. E. Roberts and H. T. Duong, "The Prospective Association Between Sleep Deprivation and Depression Among Adolescents," *Sleep: Journal of Sleep and Sleep Disorders Research* 37 (2014): 239–244.

8 *Half of teens said they were online "almost constantly" by 2022*: E. A. Vogels, R. Gelles-Watnick, and N. Massarat, *Teens, Social Media, and Technology 2022*, Pew Research Center. August 10, 2022.

8 *2023, according to Gallup, the average American teen spent almost five hours a day using social media*: J. Rothwell, "Teens Spend Average of 4.8 Hours on Social Media Per Day," Gallup, October 1, 2023.

8 *Around the world, more teens said they felt lonely at school starting around 2012*: J. M. Twenge et al., "Worldwide Increases in Adolescent Loneliness," *Journal of Adolescence* 93 (2021): 257–269.

8 *In Europe and English-speaking countries, rates of anxiety and depression also spiked among teens after 2012*: M. Boer et al., "National-Level Schoolwork Pressure, Family Structure, Internet Use, and Obesity as Drivers of Time Trends

in Adolescent Psychological Complaints Between 2002 and 2018," *Journal of Youth and Adolescence* 52 (2023): 2061–2077; P. Patalay and S. H. Gage, "Changes in Millennial Adolescent Mental Health and Health-Related Behaviours over 10 Years: A Population Cohort Comparison Study," *International Journal of Epidemiology* 48 (2019): 1650–1664.; N. Pavic et al., "Social Media and the Decline in Australian Youth Mental Health Outcomes," manuscript under review, 2025.

8 *The number of 10- to 14-year-old girls admitted to the emergency room for self-harm in the U.S. quintupled*: J. M. Twenge, *Generations: The Real Differences Between Gen Z, Millennials, Gen X, Boomers and Silents—and What They Mean for America's Future* (New York: Atria Books, 2025), Figure 6.36.

8 *twice as many 10- to 14-year-olds took their own lives via suicide*: Twenge, *Generations*, Figure 6.38.

9 *heavy users of social media were three times as likely to be depressed as nonusers*: Y. Kelly, A. Zilanawala, C. Booker, and A. Sacker, "Social Media Use and Adolescent Mental Health: Findings from the UK Millennium Cohort Study," *EClinical Medicine*, 2019.

9 *Across dozens of studies, teens who are heavy users of screen media (electronic games, the internet, online videos, and social media) are between 30% and 200% more likely*: M. Liu et al., "Time Spent on Social Media and Risk of Depression in Adolescents: A Dose-Response Meta-Analysis, *International Journal of Environmental Research and Public Health* 19, no. 9 (2022); E. Messias et al., "Sadness, Suicide, and Their Association with Video Game and Internet Overuse Among Teens: Results from the Youth Risk Behavior Survey 2007 and 2009," *Suicide and Life-Threatening Behavior* 41 (2011): 307–315; J. M. Twenge and E. Farley, "Not All Screen Time Is Created Equal: Associations with Mental Health Vary by Activity and Gender," *Social Psychiatry and Psychiatric Epidemiology* 56 (2021): 207-217; J. M. Twenge and W. K. Campbell, "Digital Media Use Is Linked to Lower Psychological Well-Being: Evidence from Three Datasets," *Psychiatric Quarterly* 90 (2019): 311–331.

10 *When people cut back on social media for a few weeks, they end up happier and less depressed compared to those who keep using social media as they always have*: H. Allcott, L. Braghieri, S. Eichmeyer, and M. Gentzkow, "The Welfare Effects of Social Media," *American Economic Review* 110 (2020): 629–676; M. G. Hunt, R. Marx, C. Lipson, and J. Young, "No More FOMO: Limiting Social Media Decreases Loneliness and Depression," *Journal of Social and Clinical Psychology* 37 (2018): 751–768.

10 *after two weeks with minimal access to screens, kids and teens were less angry and less depressed compared to a control group*: J. Schmidt-Persson et al., "Screen Media Use and Mental Health of Children and Adolescents: A Secondary Analysis of a Randomized Clinical Trial," *JAMA Network Open* 7 (2024): e2419881.

11 *the U.S. Surgeon General called for warning labels to be placed on social media*: V. H. Murthy, "Surgeon General: Why I'm Calling for a Warning Label on Social Media Platforms," *New York Times*, June 17, 2024.

11 *When Alexis Spence was 11, she opened an Instagram account on her iPad*: J. Cook, "Family Sues Meta, Blames Instagram for Daughter's Eating Disorder and Self-Harm, NBCNews.com, June 7, 2022.

11 *A blackmailer posing as a teen girl talked a 15-year-old Utah boy*: Carmen Nesbitt, "After an Online 'Sextortion' Threat, a Utah Teen Died by Suicide. Now His Parents Are Warning Others," *Salt Lake Tribune*, April 20, 2024.

11 *Selena Rodriquez opened an Instagram account when she was 10*: A. Suliman, "Mother of 11-Year-Old Who Died by Suicide Sues Social Media Firms Meta and Snap," *Washington Post*, January 22, 2022.

12 *but cyberbullying, pornography, sexual exploitation, references to drugs, and other dangers persist*: "Venezuela Court Fines TikTok $10 Million over Deadly Challenges," Bloomberg News, December 30, 2024; M. B. Robb and S. Mann, *Teens and Pornography* (San Francisco, CA: Common Sense, 2023); J. Horwitz, "Snap Failed to Warn Users About Sextortion Risks, State Lawsuit Alleges," *Wall Street Journal*, October 1, 2024; M. Elsen-Rooney, "More Bullying, Teacher Dissatisfaction with the Chancellor: 5 Takeaways from NYC's 2024 School Survey, *Chalkbeat New York*, August 30, 2024.

12 *According to Snapchat's own research, one in four 13- to 15-year-olds have been asked to share explicit pictures*: "New Snap Research: Gen Z Remains a Target for Online Sextortion, But Signs of Progress," Snap, Inc., October 29, 2024.

12 *"There is no seatbelt for parents to click"*: V. H. Murthy, "Surgeon General: Why I'm Calling for a Warning Label on Social Media Platforms," *New York Times*, June 17, 2024.

15 *The prefrontal cortex, which is in charge of self-control and decision-making, develops more slowly than the rest of the brain*: S. M. Kolk and P. Rakic, "Development of Prefrontal Cortex," *Neuropsychopharmacology* 47 (2021): 41–57.

16 *"My job as their dad is to be their prefrontal cortex until it shows up"*: S. Galloway, Age Gating. *No Mercy/No Malice*, June 28, 2024.

16 *"you're exploiting a vulnerability in human psychology"*: E. Pandey, "Sean Parker: Facebook Was Designed to Exploit Human 'Vulnerability,'" *Axios*, November 9, 2017.

17 *concluded that minors have "minimal ability to self-regulate effectively"*: State of Nebraska v. TikTok Inc., Case No. CI 24-1759, page 11, paragraph 76.

RULE 1: YOU'RE IN CHARGE

19 *On average, kids now get their first smartphones around age 11*: S. McMacken, States where kids get smartphones earliest, Secure Data Recovery, September 6, 2024.

19 *38% of 10- to 12-year-olds use social media*: V. Rideout, A. Peebles, S. Mann, M. B. Robb, *Common Sense Census: Media Use by Tweens and Teens, 2021* (San Francisco, CA: Common Sense, 2022).

21 *The "dolphin" label comes from authoritative parents being firm but flexible, like the body of a dolphin*: S. K. Kang, *The Dolphin Parent: A Guide to Raising Healthy, Happy, and Self-Motivated Kids* (New York: Viking, 2014).

22 *The research is clear that authoritative (dolphin) parenting works the best and leads to the most well-adjusted children*: J. Hayek et al., "Authoritative Parenting Stimulates Academic Achievement, Also Partly via Self-Efficacy and Intention Towards Getting Good Grades," *PLOS ONE* 17 (2022) : 1–20; S. Kuppens and E. Ceulemans, "Parenting Styles: A Closer Look at a Well-Known Concept," *Journal of Child & Family Studies* 28 (2019): 168–181; M. Lavrič and A. Naterer, "The Power of Authoritative Parenting: A Cross-National Study of Effects of Exposure to Different Parenting Styles on Life Satisfaction," *Children and Youth Services Review* 116 (2020).

22 *"One of my main jobs is to make decisions that I think are good for you"*: B. Kennedy, "It's Time to Set Boundaries," *Time*, November 11, 2024.

23 *half of 18- to 27-year-olds said they wished TikTok and Snapchat had never been invented*: B. Greenfield, "Nearly Half of Gen Z'ers Wish Tiktok 'Was Never Invented,' Survey Finds," *Fortune*, September 17, 2024.

24 *Nearly 6 out of 10 young adults think parents should not give children smartphones before high school*: A. J. Skiera, "What Gen Z Thinks About Its Social Media and Smartphone Usage," Harris Poll, September 10, 2024.

24 *"Why do parents give their children smartphones?" asked middle school student*: A. Trivedi, "Smartphone Addiction: One Middle Schooler's Perspective," Stone Soup blogs, May 30, 2022.

24 *UK journalist Decca Aitkenhead asked sisters Edie, 15, and Rose, 13*: D. Aitkenhead, "What Happened When I Made My Sons and Their Friends Go Without Smartphones," *Sunday Times*, August 18, 2024.

25 *the platform has allowed adults to blackmail teens into attempting suicide (which, unfortunately, it has)*: S. Boburg, P. Verma, and C. Dehghanpoor, "On Popular Online Platforms, Predatory Groups Coerce Children into Self-Harm," *Washington Post*, March 13, 2024.

32 *"who always has the right to return to base should the skies be more turbulent"*: Kennedy, "It's Time to Set Boundaries."

RULE 2: NO ELECTRONIC DEVICES IN THE BEDROOM OVERNIGHT

35 *Diana heard her daughter talking and went to investigate*: D. Park, "I Took My Teens' Cell Phones Away at Night—and Noticed a Huge Difference," *Scary Mommy*, December 16, 2021.

35 *6 out of 10 kids used their phones between midnight and 5 a.m. on school nights in a study that tracked 11- to 17-year-olds' phone use*: J. S. Radesky, H. M. Weeks, A. Schaller, M. B. Robb, S. Mann, and A. Lenhart, *Constant Companion: A Week in the Life of a Young Person's Smartphone Use* (San Francisco, CA: Common Sense, 2023).

35 *"Sometimes I look up and it's 3 a.m. and I'm watching a video of a giraffe"*: L. Holson, "Social Media's Vampires: They Text by Night," *New York Times*, July 3, 2014.

36 *Yet most kids—90% according to one study—are not getting enough sleep*: E. Draper, "Bedtime Study: Let Sleeping Kids Lie; 90% Sleep Deprived," *Denver Post*, June 9, 2016.

36 *And if they are waking up in the middle of the night to use their phones, as a third of teens admitted to in one survey*: B. Morris, "Many Teens Check Their Phones in Middle of Night," *Wall Street Journal*, May 29, 2019.

37 *When parents enforce bedtimes, studies find teens get nearly a half hour more sleep*: M. A. Short, M. Gradisar, L. C. Lack, H. R. Wright, J. F. Dewald, A. R. Wolfson, M. A. Carskadon, (2013). "A Cross-Cultural Comparison of Sleep Duration Between US and Australian Adolescents: The Effect of School Start Time, Parent-Set Bedtimes, and Extracurricular Load," *Health Education & Behavior* 40 (2013): 323–330.

37 *Teens whose parents let them stay up until midnight were 24% more likely to suffer from depression*: J. E. Gangwisch, L. A. Babiss, D. Malaspina, D., J. B. Turner, G. K. Zammit, and K. Posner, "Earlier Parental Set Bedtimes as a Protective Factor Against Depression and Suicidal Ideation," *Sleep: Journal of Sleep and Sleep Disorders Research* 33 (2010): 97–106.

39 *28% of 12- and 13-year-olds used their phones when they woke up during the night*: J. M. Nagata, C. M. Cheng, J. Shim, O. Kiss, K. T. Ganson, A. Testa, J. He, and F. C. Baker, "Bedtime Screen Use Behaviors and Sleep Outcomes in Early Adolescents: A Prospective Cohort Study," *Journal of Adolescent Health* 75 (2024): 650–655.

39 *Decades of research have found that kids who have a TV or gaming console*: O. Bruni, S. Sette, L. Fontanesi, R. Baiocco, F. Laghi, and E. Baumgartner, "Technology Use and Sleep Quality in Preadolescence and Adolescence," *Journal of Clinical Sleep Medicine* 11 (2015): 1433–1441; D. A. Gentile, O. N. Berch, H. Choo, A. Khoo, and D. A. Walsh, "Bedroom Media: One Risk Factor for Development," *Developmental Psychology* 53 (2017): 2340–2355; and A. F. Helm and R. M. C. Spencer, "Television Use and Its Effects on Sleep in Early Childhood," *Sleep Health* 5 (2019): 241–247.

41 *Kids who used their devices right before sleep, compared to those who didn't, were 44% more likely to not sleep enough*: B. Carter, P. Rees, L. Hale, D. Bhattacharjee, and M. S. Paradkar, "Association Between Portable Screen-Based

Media Device Access or Use and Sleep Outcomes: A Systematic Review and Meta-Analysis," *JAMA Pediatrics*, 170 (2016): 1202–1208.

41 *In another study, 11- to 14-year-olds slept nearly a half hour less*: B. Brosnan, J. J. Haszard, K. A. Meredith-Jones, S.-R. Wickham, B. C. Galland, and RW. Taylor, "Screen Use at Bedtime and Sleep Duration and Quality Among Youths," *JAMA Pediatrics* 178 (2024): 1147–1154.

RULE 3: NO SOCIAL MEDIA UNTIL AGE 16—OR LATER

49 *it was a compromise politicians reached with tech companies in 1998 at the dawn of the internet*: Federal Trade Commission, Children's Online Privacy Protection Rule ("COPPA"), 1998, 15 U.S.C. 6501-6505.

50 *The limbic (emotional) system is on high alert, the prefrontal cortex (self-control) is less developed, and the two areas do not communicate as well*: A. Solomon, "Doom Scrolling," *New Yorker*, October 7, 2024.

51 *68% of 11- and 12-year-olds—none of whom are legally allowed to have accounts—freely admit to using social media*: J. S. Radesky et al., *Constant Companion: A Week in the Life of a Young Person's Smartphone Use* (San Francisco, CA: Common Sense, 2023).

51 *three out of four parents said they regretted*: E. Parker, "Screen Time Dilemma: When Should Kids Get Their First Smartphone?," The Harris Poll, June 26, 2024.

52 *One in five 13- to 15-year-old girls have been sexually propositioned via social media. Even more, 37%, report being exposed to unwanted nudity*: E. Terry, "Big Tech Asked to Support Child Safety Legislation During Hearing on Child Sexual Exploitation," *Deseret News*, February 1, 2024.

52 *The majority of teen girls who use Instagram or Snapchat have been contacted on the app by a stranger who made them uncomfortable*: J. Nesi, S. Mann, and M. B. Robb, *Teens and Mental Health: How Girls Really Feel About Social Media* (San Francisco, CA: Common Sense, 2023).

52 *Snapchat alone has received more than 10,000 reports of sextortion a* month: J. Horwitz, "Snap Failed to Warn Users About Sextortion Risks, State Lawsuit Alleges," *Wall Street Journal*, October 1, 2024.

52 *When a U.S. senator's staffers opened a test account on Instagram as a 13-year-old girl*: K. Rosenblatt, "Senator's Office Posed as a Girl on Fake Instagram Account to Study App's Effect," NBCNews.com, September 30, 2021.

53 *About half of young adults say they've seen at least one self-harm post on Instagram*: F. Arendt, S. Scherr, and D. Romer, "Effects of Exposure to Self-Harm On Social Media: Evidence from a Two-Wave Panel Study Among Young Adults," *New Media & Society* 21 (2019): 2422–2442.

53 *UK teen Molly Russell's Instagram delivered more than 300 posts a month related to suicide, self-harm, and depression*: C. Dyer, "Social Media Content Con-

tributed to Teenager's Death 'In More Than a Minimal Way,' Says Coroner," *BMJ* 379 (October 3, 2022): o2374; A. Crawford, "Molly Russell: Tech Firms Still Failing After Teenager's Death, Says Father," BBC, November 29, 2023.

53 *One study found that users struggling with eating disorders (versus those who were not) were shown 146% more appearance-oriented videos*: S. Griffiths et al., "Does TikTok Contribute to Eating Disorders? A Comparison of the TikTok Algorithms Belonging to Individuals with Eating Disorders Versus Healthy Controls," *Body Image* 51(2024): 101807.

53 *Danish researchers created fake Instagram profiles that shared self-harm content*: M. Bryant, "Instagram Actively Helping Spread of Self-Harm Among Teenagers, Study Finds," *Guardian*, November 30, 2024.

54 *The TikTok feed of Chase Nasca, 16, grew increasingly dark in the early days of 2022*: O. Carville, "TikTok's Algorithm Keeps Pushing Suicide to Vulnerable Kids," *Bloomberg* Businessweek, April 20, 2023.

57 *Meta's own research describes the "grief spiral" teen girls go through when they compare themselves to others on the platform*: *Wall Street Journal* Staff, "Teen Girls Body Image and Social Comparison on Instagram—An Exploratory Study in the US. Facebook's Documents About Instagram and Teens, Published," *Wall Street Journal*, September 29, 2021.

57 *"I never felt like I looked good enough in my photos"*: A. Mendes, *#Unsubscribed: How I Am Thriving in High School Without Social Media (And You Can, Too)* (2019).

57 *the strongest associations were for girls between the ages of 12 and 15*: A. Orben, A. K. Przybylski, S. J. Blakemore, and R. A. Kievit, "Windows of Developmental Sensitivity to Social Media," *Nature Communications* 13 (2022): 1649.

60 *"Teens . . . often feel 'addicted' and know that what they're seeing is bad for their mental health"*: G. Wells, J. Horwitz, and D. Seetharaman, "Facebook Knows Instagram Is Toxic for Teen Girls, Company Documents Show," *Wall Street Journal*, September 14, 2021.

60 *Nearly 6 out of 10 of people—including Instagram users themselves—said they would prefer to live in a world without Instagram*: L. Bursztyn, B. Handel, R. Jimenez-Duran, and C. Roth, "When Product Markets Become Collective Traps: The Case of Social Media," Becker Friedman Institute, University of Chicago, October 3, 2023.

60 *After 20 minutes of watching Reels, the accounts' feeds filled with ads from sex content creators*: J. Horwitz, "Instagram Recommends Sexual Videos to Accounts for 13-Year-Olds, Tests Show," *Wall Street Journal*, June 20, 2024.

61 *13% of British users and 6% of American users who had suicidal thoughts said their desire to kill themselves traced back to Instagram*: Wells, Horwitz, and Seetharaman, "Facebook Knows Instagram Is Toxic for Teen Girls."

61 *The app fed Englyn Roberts, 14, a post of a woman who screamed and pretended to hang herself with an electrical cord*: K. Nelson, "Teen Watched Simulated Hanging Video on Instagram Before Suicide," *60 Minutes* Overtime, December 11, 2022.

61 *A third of teens say they use it "almost constantly"*: M. Faverio and O. Sidoti, "Teens, Social Media, and Technology," Pew Research Center, December 12, 2024.

61 *On TikTok, I'd see prettier girls than me and it would make me more upset*: K. Robinson, "Northern Kentucky Family Shares Story of Their Teen's Online Addiction," WKRC, Local 12, May 20, 2021.

62 *TikTok's internal research concluded that 100% of content "fetishizing minors" leaked through its moderation process, as did half of content glorifying the sexual assault of minors*: Haidt, J. and Rausch, Z. "TikTok Is Harming Children at an Industrial Scale," *After Babel* Substack, January 9, 2025.

62 *When* The Wall Street Journal *created fake accounts for 13-year-olds*: R. Barry, G. Wells, J. West, and J. Stern "How TikTok Serves Up Sex and Drug Videos to Minors," *Wall Street Journal*, September 8, 2021.

62 *Apple told TikTok to rate the app as 17+ on the App Store, but TikTok refused and kept it listed as 12+*: C. Lima-Strong, "Apple Told TikTok It's Unfit for Young Teens, New Lawsuit Details Allege," *Washington Post*, October 31, 2024.

62 *Blackout challenge, has led to the deaths of at least 20 children, including 9- and 10-year-olds*: A. R. Sarkar, "TikTok's 'Blackout' Challenge Linked to Deaths of 20 Children in 18 Months, Report Says," *Independent*, December 1, 2022.

62 *The Chroming challenge involves inhaling toxic fumes*: A. Johnson, "What Is 'Chroming?' UK Boy Dies After Participating in 'Dangerous' Social Media Challenge," *Forbes*, March 8, 2024.

62 *The Skullbreaker challenge encourages kids to trick someone*: M. Burke, "TikTok 'Skull-Breaker Challenge' Lands New Jersey Boy, 13, in Hospital, 2 Charged," NBCNews.com, March 3, 2020.

62 *The Devious Licks challenge led to students destroying school property across the country*: J. Doubek, "Students Are Damaging School Bathrooms for Attention on TikTok," NPR, September 17, 2021.

63 *The company's internal research found that half a million Snapchat users a day were exposed to drug-related content*: O. Carville, "Fentanyl Almost Killed Michael Brewer. Now He Wants Snap to Pay," *Bloomberg Businessweek*, December 19, 2024.

63 *The families of 64 young people who died from fentanyl overdoses sued the company*: Carville, "Fentanyl Almost Killed Michael Brewer"; D. Tolentino and K. Snow, "Judge Allows Lawsuit Against Snap from Relatives of Dead Children to Move Forward," NBCNews.com, January 3, 2024.

64 *A man on a Discord server persuaded a 14-year-old girl to send him a nude picture of herself*: S. Boburg, P. Verma, and C. Dehghanpoor, "On Popular Online Platforms, Predatory Groups Coerce Children into Self-Harm," *Washington Post*, March 13, 2024.

65 *In one study of almost 500 teens, using WhatsApp*: A. Van der Wal, I. Beyens, L. H. C. Janssen and P. M. Valkenburg, "Social Media Use Leads to Negative Mental Health Outcomes for Most Adolescents," preprint manuscript, PsyArXiv, 2025.

66 *Alexis Spence, who we met in the introduction, got her own tablet at 11*: J. Cook, "Family Sues Meta, Blames Instagram for Daughter's Eating Disorder and Self-Harm," NBCNews.com, June 7, 2022.

68 *social media companies make $11 billion a year in advertising revenue from children and teens 17 and under:* A. Raffoul et al., "Social Media Platforms Generate Billions of Dollars in Revenue from U.S. Youth: Findings from a Simulated Revenue Model," *PLOS One* 18 (2023): e0295337.

68 *"the lifetime value of a 13 y/o teen is roughly $270 per teen"*: J. Horwitz, "Meta Designed Products to Capitalize on Teen Vulnerabilities, States Allege," *Wall Street Journal*, November 25, 2023.

70 *LGBTQ+ teens who are heavy users of social media are more likely to be depressed*: D. Klinger et al., "Exploring the Relationship Between Media Use and Depressive Symptoms Among Gender Diverse Youth: Findings of the Mental Health Days Study," *Child and Adolescent Psychiatry and Mental Health* 18 (2024).

70 *LGBTQ+ young adults are more likely to say the impact of social media on their emotional health was negative*: J. Haidt and W. Johnson, "Gen Z Has Regrets," *New York Times*, September 17, 2024.

71 *TikTok's own internal research concluded that their parental controls (Family Pairing) did not protect kids from sexual content*: *State of Nebraska v. TikTok Inc.*, Case No. CI 24-1759, page 61, paragraph 198.

71 *A 2025 report found that Instagram teen accounts*: Accountable Tech, *Scary Feeds: The Reality of Teen Accounts*, May 2025. G. Fowler, "Gen Z Users and a Dad Tested Instagram Teen Accounts. Their Feeds Were Shocking," *Washington Post*, May 18, 2025.

RULE 4: FIRST PHONES SHOULD BE BASIC PHONES

73 *Logan Lane got her first smartphone*: L. Garcia-Navarro, "The Teenager Leading the Smartphone Liberation Movement," *New York Times* First Person podcast, February 2, 2023.

74 *Every single activity on a screen was linked to more unhappiness, and every single activity that didn't involve a screen was instead linked to less unhappiness*: J. M. Twenge, *iGen: Why Today's Super-Connected Kids Are Growing Up Less*

Rebellious, More Tolerant, Less Happy—and Completely Unprepared for Adulthood (New York: Atria Books, 2017).

76 *Well yes, Martinko argues, he's missing spending all his leisure time on screens*: K. Martinko, "My Teenaged Son Still Doesn't Have a Smartphone. Here's Why," *Globe and Mail*, August 28, 2024; K. J. Martinko, *Childhood Unplugged: Practical Advice to Get Kids Off Screens and Find Balance* (Gabriola Island, BC, Canada: New Society Publishers, 2023).

78 *adults who gave up internet access on their phone for a month*: N. Castelo, K. Kushlev, A. F. Ward, M. Esterman, and P. B. Reiner, "Blocking Mobile Internet on Smartphones Improves Sustained Attention, Mental Health, and Subjective Well-Being," *PNAS Nexus* 4 (February 2025): pgaf017.

RULE 5: GIVE THE FIRST SMARTPHONE WITH THE DRIVER'S LICENSE

91 *"I wish I hadn't. If I could go back and do it over, I'd delay even longer"*: K. J. Martinko, "When should I give my kid a phone?," *The Analog Family*, Substack, May 31, 2023.

92 *The later a young person got their first smartphone, the better their mental health in young adulthood*: "Age of first smartphone/tablet and mental well-being outcomes," Sapien Labs, May 15, 2023.

94 *Kids 11 to 17 get an average of 237 notifications a* day: J. S. Radesky et al., *Constant Companion: A Week in the Life of a Young Person's Smartphone Use* (San Francisco, CA: Common Sense, 2023).

RULE 6: USE PARENTAL CONTROLS

98 *when parents monitor device use, kids are much less likely to be heavy users*: I. M. Koning, M. Peeters, C. Finkenauer, and R. J. J. M. Van Den Eijnden, "Bidirectional Effects of Internet-Specific Parenting Practices and Compulsive Social Media and Internet Game Use," *Journal of Behavioral Addictions* 7 (2018): 624–632; L. Paakkari, J. Tynjälä, H. Lahti, K. Ojala, and N. Lyyra, "Problematic Social Media Use and Health Among Adolescents," *International Journal of Environmental Research and Public Health* 18 (2021).

98 *and are also less likely to suffer from depression, dissatisfaction with life, or insecurity about their appearance*: J. Fardouly et al., "Parental Control of the Time Preadolescents Spend on Social Media: Links with Preadolescents' Social Media Appearance Comparisons and Mental Health," *Journal of Youth and Adolescence* 47 (2018): 1456–1468.

98 *A set of studies found that parents who used parental control software were less stressed and happier*: L. Bertrandias, Y. Bernard, and L. Elgaaied-Gambier, "How Using Parental Control Software Can Enhance Parents' Well-Being: The

Role of Product Features on Parental Efficacy and Stress," *Journal of Interactive Marketing* 58 (2023): 280–300.

105 *"I quickly realized Apple's parental controls aren't the panacea they're promised to be"*: J. Horwitz and A. Tilley, "Apple Helped Nix Part of a Child Safety Bill. More Fights Are Expected," *Wall Street Journal*, September 2, 2024.

RULE 7: CREATE NO-PHONE ZONES

114 *kids who use devices in bed before they go to sleep don't sleep as well or as long*: B. Carter et al., "Association Between Portable Screen-Based Media Device Access or Use and Sleep Outcomes: A Systematic Review and Meta-Analysis, *JAMA Pediatrics* 170 (2016): 1202–1208.

114 *College students who used devices for an hour before bed were 59% more likely to have symptoms of insomnia*: G. J. Hjetland, J. C. Skogen, M. Hysing, M. Gradisar, and B. Sivertsen, "How and When Screens Are Used: Comparing Different Screen Activities and Sleep in Norwegian University Students," *Frontiers in Psychiatry* 16 (2025): 1548273.

114 *"For certain apps, like TikTok, it's really hard to fall asleep once you use it close to when you're gonna go to sleep"*: J. S. Radesky et al., *Constant Companion: A Week in the Life of a Young Person's Smartphone Use* (San Francisco, CA: Common Sense, 2023).

116 *those without their phones enjoyed the dinner more*: R. J. Dwyer, K. Kushlev, and E. W. Dunn, "Smartphone Use Undermines Enjoyment of Face-to-Face Social Interactions," *Journal of Experimental Social Psychology* 78 (2018): 233–239.

116 *setting phones aside during everyday conversations results in an even larger increase in enjoyment and happiness than phone-free dinners*: Dwyer, Kushlev, and Dunn, "Smartphone Use Undermines Enjoyment."

116 phubbing *(it's a combination of* phone *and* snubbing*). Everyone hates phubbing*: E. Barrick, A. Barasch, and D. I. Tamir, "The Unexpected Social Consequences of Diverting Attention to Our Phones," *Journal of Experimental Social Psychology* 101 (2022): 1–14.

118 *their social skills were better than their peers who hadn't gone to camp yet*: Y. T. Uhls et al., "Five Days at Outdoor Education Camp Without Screens Improves Preteen Skills with Nonverbal Emotion Cues," *Computers in Human Behavior* 39 (2014): 387–392.

118 *Teens who spent two weeks at a Scout camp developed more self-control, empathy, and self-confidence*: E. Kirchhoff, R. Keller, and B. Blanc, "Empowering Young People—The Impact of Camp Experiences on Personal Resources, Well-Being, and Community Building," *Frontiers in Psychology* 15 (2024); L. Mygind et al., "Mental, Physical and Social Health Benefits of Immersive Nature-Experience for Children and Adolescents: A Systematic Review and Quality Assessment of the Evidence, *Health & Place* 58 (2019).

119 *As an* Atlantic *article recently put it, "To read a book in college, it helps if you read a book in high school"*: R. Horowitch, "The Elite College Students Who Can't Read Books," *Atlantic*, October 1, 2024.

119 *In recent years, 40% of high school seniors have not read a single book in the last year that wasn't assigned for school*: J. M. Twenge, G. N. Martin, and B. H. Spitzberg, "Trends in U.S. Adolescents' Media Use, 1976-2016: The Rise of Digital Media, the Decline of TV, and the (Near) Demise of Print," *Psychology of Popular Media Culture* 8 (2019): 329–345.

122 *device use also leads to boredom*: J. Dora et al., "Fatigue, Boredom and Objectively Measured Smartphone Use at Work," *Royal Society Open Science* 8 (2021): 201915.

122 *people who had their phones available during conversations with friends were more likely to say they were bored*: R. J. Dwyer, K. Kushlev, and E. W. Dunn, "Smartphone Use Undermines Enjoyment of Face-to-Face Social Interactions," *Journal of Experimental Social Psychology* 78 (2018): 233–239.

123 *digital app switching led to more boredom, not less*: K. Y. Y. Tam and M. Inzlicht, "Fast-Forward to Boredom: How Switching Behavior on Digital Media Makes People More Bored," *Journal of Experimental Psychology: General* 153 (2024): 2409–2426.

RULE 8: GIVE YOUR KIDS REAL-WORLD FREEDOM

125 *"The mood is electric," with the teens gushing about how much fun they had*: D. Aitkenhead, "What Happened When I Made My Sons and Their Friends Go Without Smartphones," *Sunday Times*, August 18, 2024.

126 *fewer have their driver's license, go out on dates, or work at paid jobs than in previous generations*: J. M. Twenge and H. Park, "The Decline in Adult Activities Among U.S. Adolescents, 1976–2016," *Child Development* 90 (2019): 638–654.

129 *One study found that when parents hear that independent activities are teachable moments*: M. Cummings, "Need a Landing Pad for Helicopter Parenting? Frame Tasks as Learning," *Yale News*, November 22, 2024.

131 *One study had clinically anxious kids do new things on their own almost every day for four weeks*: C. Ortiz and M. Fastman, "A Novel Independence Intervention to Treat Child Anxiety: A Nonconcurrent Multiple Baseline Evaluation," *Journal of Anxiety Disorders* 105 (2024): 102893.

132 *In a 2023 poll, only 50% of parents of kids ages 9 to 11*: Mott Poll Report: Promoting children's independence: What parents say vs. do. National Poll on Children's Health, C. S. Mott Children's Hospital, October 16, 2023.

133 *When Let Grow founder Lenore Skenazy's son was nine, he begged her to let him take the New York subway by himself*: L. Skenazy, "Why I Let My 9-Year-Old Ride the Subway Alone," *New York Sun*, April 1, 2008.

137 *"Sleepovers, for all of their flaws, humanized others, and as a result, they made me more human too"*: E. Christakis, "The Case for Sleepovers," *Atlantic*, January 25, 2023.

138 *Even high school seniors, most of whom have a driver's license, are sticking closer to home and closer to parents these days*: J. M. Twenge, B. H. Spitzberg, and W. K. Campbell, "Less In-Person Social Interaction with Peers Among U.S. Adolescents in the 21st Century and Links to Loneliness," *Journal of Social and Personal Relationships* 36 (2019): 1892–1913.

143 *Crime is* lower *now than it was when most parents were kids in the 1970s–1990s*: J. Gramlich, "What the Data Says About Crime in the U.S.," Pew Research Center (April 24, 2024); L. Gilder, "What Latest FBI Data Shows About Violent Crime," BBC, October 18, 2024; Bureau of Justice Statistics. NCVS Dashboard, custom graphics; G. Lopez, "Crime on the Decline," *New York Times*, January 11, 2024.

143 *Stranger kidnappings are exceedingly rare*: E. Muson, "Child Abductions by Strangers Are Very Rare," *Times Union*, October 4, 2023; "Let Grow Takes a Look at Crime Statistics," LetGrow.org, December 16, 2022.

145 *"A lot of parents today are really bad at assessing risk"*: L. Skenazy, *Free-Range Kids*, 2nd edition (New York: Wiley, 2021).

146 *those who did chores scored higher on a standardized test in math*: E. M. White, M. D. DeBoer, and R. J. Scharf, "Associations Between Household Chores and Childhood Self-Competency," *Journal of Developmental and Behavioral Pediatrics* 40 (2019): 176–182.

RULE 9: BEWARE THE LAPTOP—AND THE GAMING CONSOLE, AND THE TABLET, AND . . .

156 *a Common Sense Media survey found that about 11% of teens had viewed pornography:* M. B. Robb and S. Mann, *Teens and Pornography* (San Francisco, CA: Common Sense, 2022).

RULE 10: ADVOCATE FOR NO PHONES DURING THE SCHOOL DAY

167 *"Now, you can ask them, bug them, remind them, and try to punish them, and still nothing works"*: J. Jargon, "A Teacher Did All He Could to Keep Kids Off Phones. He's Quitting in Frustration," *Wall Street Journal*, May 18, 2024.

167 *"Every day is a constant struggle against cellphone usage"*: L. Kimball, "I'm Leaving Minneapolis Schools over Cellphone Chaos: Students Can't Learn Without Enforceable Rules and Consequences," *Minneapolis Star-Tribune*, June 20, 2023.

167 *Seventy-two percent of high school teachers say that students being distracted by their phones in the classroom is a major problem*: L. Lin, K. Parker, and J. Horowitz,

"What's It Like to Be a Teacher in America Today?," Pew Research Center, April 4, 2024.

168 *the mere presence of a smartphone reduces cognitive performance*: A. F. Ward, K. Duke, A. Gneezy, and M. W. Bos, "Brain Drain: The Mere Presence of One's Own Smartphone Reduces Available Cognitive Capacity," *Journal of the Association for Consumer Research* 2 (2017): 140–154; and J. Skowronek, A. Seifert, and S. Lindberg, "The Mere Presence of a Smartphone Reduces Basal Attentional Performance," *Scientific Reports* 13 (2023): 9363.

168 *In a rural district in Colorado, more than half of the school's disciplinary issues were due to phones*: J. Jargon, "Schools Want to Ban Phones. Parents Say No," *Wall Street Journal*, April 20, 2024.

169 *When the North Adams school district in Massachusetts banned phones*: O. Banerji, "What Schools Look Like Without the Cellphone Distraction," *Education Week*, February 4, 2025.

169 *"increased student engagement in the classroom, less time spent in the bathrooms and hallways"*: J. Van Bavel, post on X/Twitter quoting school principal, March 6, 2024.

169 *A Connecticut high school reported a 35% decline in suspensions and a 50% drop in students getting sent to the principal's office*: K. C. Rohn, A. M. McCready, K. Farrell, and A. Elgoharry, "Addressing Student Technology and Social Media Use in Schools: Recommendations for School District Leaders," University of Connecticut Center for Education Policy Analysis, Research, and Evaluation, August 2024; A. Cross, "UConn Study Examines Benefits of School Phone Bans," *Government Technology*, August 19, 2024.

169 *"We had one year with a strict cellphone policy of 'if we see it, it's confiscated'"*: Kimball, "I'm leaving Minneapolis schools over cellphone chaos."

169 *"If the policy isn't clear and consistent at school, you get a slippery slope"*: Walker, "Take Cellphones Out of the Classroom."

170 *one out of four teens said they watched adult content during the school day*: Robb and Mann, *Teens and Pornography*.

170 *"In the early 1960s, when my parents were in high school, they received free sampler packs of cigarettes on their cafeteria trays"*: R. Shaw, "Why We're Banning Phones at Our School," *Atlantic*, August 4, 2024.

171 *"We're competing with Netflix"*: Walker, "Take Cellphones Out of the Classroom."

171 *A study of Norwegian middle schools found that smartphone bans led to improved academic performance*: S. Abrahamsson, "Smartphone Bans, Student Outcomes, and Mental Health," Norwegian Institute of Public Health, 2024.

171 *The vast majority of American teachers—83%—support prohibiting student phone use during the entire school day*: T. Walker, "Take Cellphones Out of the Classroom, Educators Say," *NEAToday*, October 3, 2024.

171 *"I don't want to be the phone police"*: Walker, "Take Cellphones Out of the Classroom."

172 *U.S. 8th graders' academic performance began to decline after 2012*: "Scores Decline Again for 13-Year-Old Students in Reading and Mathematics" (National Assessment of Educational Progress, 2024); A. Jones, "Math and Reading Scores for 13-Year-Olds Lowest in a Decade, Report Finds," ABCNews.com, June 21, 2023.

173 *Students with access to devices during class perform more poorly on tests, primarily because phones are so distracting*: S. Lee et al., "Cellphone Addiction Explains How Cellphones Impair Learning for Lecture Materials," *Applied Cognitive Psychology* 35 (2021): 123–135.

173 *Students who didn't have their phones scored seven percentage points higher on the test than those who kept their phones*: S. Lee et al., "The Effects of Cell Phone Use and Emotion-Regulation Style on College Students' Learning," *Applied Cognitive Psychology* 31 (2017): 360–366.

173 *A follow-up study found an even bigger difference—those without access to their phones scored 13 percentage points higher on the test*: J. S. Mendoza et al., "The Effect of Cellphones on Attention and Learning: The Influences of Time, Distraction, and Nomophobia," *Computers in Human Behavior* 86 (2018): 52–60.

174 *"I've watched students who struggle to make friends not learn how to"*: Shaw, "Why We're Banning Phones at Our School."

178 *reading on paper leads to significantly better reading comprehension than reading digitally*: P. Delgado, C. Vargas, R. Ackerman, and L. Salmerón, "Don't Throw Away Your Printed Books: A Meta-Analysis on the Effects of Reading Media on Reading Comprehension," *Educational Research Review* 25 (2018): 23–38.

178 *U.S. 4th and 8th graders who spent more time using digital devices in language arts classes performed worse on reading tests*: L. Salmerón, C. Vargas, P. Delgado, and N. Baron, "Relation Between Digital Tool Practices in the Language Arts Classroom and Reading Comprehension Scores," *Reading and Writing: An Interdisciplinary Journal* 36 (2023): 175–194.

178 *College students who took handwritten notes were 58% more likely to get A's in college courses*: A. E. Flanigan et al., "Typed Versus Handwritten Lecture Notes and College Student Achievement: A Meta-Analysis," *Educational Psychology Review* 36 (2024).

179 *Students lasted an average of six minutes studying on their laptops before they started browsing social media or texting*: L. D. Rosen, M. L. Carrier, and N. A. Cheever, "Facebook and Texting Made Me Do It: Media-Induced Task-Switching While Studying," *Computers in Human Behavior* 29 (2013): 948–958.

179 *child starting school in this decade won't retire until the 2080s:* A. Tyson, "The False Promise of Device-Based Education," *After Babel*, Substack, October 17, 2024.

180 *"often sound very supportive of cellphone policies and want their kids to learn, but they also want access to them at all times"*: Jargon, "Schools Want to Ban Phones."

180 *"School is supposed to be a place where students get distance"*: L. Shulman, "The Parent in My Classroom: How My Students Stay Tethered, via FaceTime and Email, to Their Homes," *Slate*, March 9, 2024.

181 *School safety experts agree that students having phones during a shooting is actually* more *dangerous*: E. Chuck, "Lifeline or Distraction? Georgia Shooting Reignites Debate over Cellphones in Schools," NBCNews.com, September 7, 2024; H. Kelly, "Even After Shootings, Experts Warn Against Cellphones in Schools," *Washington Post*, June 1, 2022; S. H. Murray, "That's a Long Half Hour for a Parent," *Slate*, June 9, 2024; and M. Kyle, "Schools and Cellphones: The Added Danger They Can Pose in Emergency Situations," WKYC.com, May 9, 2024.

INDEX

academic performance, 171–74, 178
addiction
  to Instagram, 60
  to Snapchat, 63
  to social media, 16, 49, 97
  to TikTok, 61
Advocate for No Phones During the School Day (Rule 10), 167–82
  academic consequences of school phone policies, 171–74
  advocate for low-tech schools, 178–79
  common obstacles and pushbacks, 179–82
  goals of, 168–71
  parents' ability to effect policy change, 175–78
  social consequences of phones in school, 174–75
affection, in parenting styles, 20–23
age-gating, 15–16
Aitkenhead, Decca, 24, 125–26, 143
alarm clock, using phone as, 45
algorithms, 16–17, 71
  disturbing content promoted by, 54
  harmful content promoted by, 52–53
  to maximize engagement, 55–56
  of problematic platforms, 59
  "sticky" nature of, 99
  of TikTok, 61
  of X/Twitter, 64
  of YouTube, 65, 156
Android phone controls, 104, 106
And the Band Played On (Shilts), 120
anger, screen media use and, 10
anxiety, 8
  and independence, 130–31, 147
  of parents, about school phone bans, 180–82
Anxious Generation, The (Haidt), 128, 152
Apple, 105
  parental controls of, 158–61
  and TikTok age rating, 62
Apple Watches, 80
appointments, making, 142
apps
  to allow, 59, 83–85
  for basic phones, 83–85
  blocking downloads of, 98–99, 153, 155
  keeping kids off of, 59
  maximizing engagement on, 55–56
  to not allow, 59–65
  to possibly allow, 65–66
  selective blocking of, 101
  uninstalling and reinstalling, 99
  see also individual apps

Aura, 105
authoritarian parenting (tiger shark parenting), 20–22
authoritative parenting (dolphin parenting), 20–23
  see also You're in Charge (Rule 1)
Away for the Day program, 176, 177

Bark parental control software, 105
Bark phone, 82
basic phones, 14, 78, 80
  apps to allow on, 83–85
  choosing, 79–83
  types of, 81–83
  see also First Phones Should Be Basic Phones (Rule 4)
Beccaccio, Abbigail, 64
bedtimes
  exceptions to, 38
  to get enough sleep, 37
  importance of, 37–39
  no-phone zone before, 114–15
  parental controls for, 101
  see also No Electronic Devices in the Bedroom Overnight (Rule 2)
Beware the Laptop—and the Gaming Console, and the Tablet, and . . . (Rule 9), 149–66
  Apple's parental controls, 158–61
  common obstacles and pushbacks, 165–66
  gaming consoles, 151–55
  kids' amount of screen time overall, 164–65
  laptop parental controls, 161–64
  personal laptops, 157–58
  school laptops, 155–57
  tablets, 150–51
blackmailers, 11, 25, 52, 63, 64
Blackout challenge, 62
Black teens, social media use by, 70
blocking app downloads, 98–99, 153, 155
blue light, 40–41, 115
body, information about, 31
body image issues, 57, 60
boredom, 121–23
boundary setting, 22–23, 26–28
brain, in adolescence, 50
brain rot, 25
Brewer, Michael, 63–64
building things, 138

Cairns, Warwick, 144–45
camping, 117–19, 136, 143
Canopy, 105
Carver, Kim, 105
cat videos, 54
"challenges," TikTok, 62
chat rooms, blocking access to, 102
Chess for Kids, 84
Christakis, Erika, 136–37
Chroming challenge, 62
circadian rhythm, 37, 40
clubs, social media posts of, 69–70
combination lockboxes, 43
competition, for likes/followers, 54, 59
content
  disturbing, 54
  drug, 62
  harmful, 52–54, 60
  on problematic platforms, 59
  sexual, 62, 64–65
  toxic, 65
  violent, 65, 102
conversations with kids, *see* talking with kids
cooking, helping with, 137
COVID-19 pandemic, 8
Create No-Phone Zones (Rule 7), 113–23

before bedtime, 114–15
camps and outside time, 117–19
common obstacles and pushbacks, 121–23
face-to-face conversations, 116–17
family dinners, 116
summer or weekend downtime, 119–20
vacations, 117
creativity, 128–29
credit cards, 132–33, 143
crime rates, 143–45
cruel texts or comments, 31, 55
cyberbullying, 55, 65, 70, 168, 169

damaging experiences with social media, 51–59
dating, 126–28
dating sites, blocking access to, 102
decision-making skills, 90–91, 127–28
depression
changing trends in, 5, 6, 8, 9
and device use, 9
and gaming, 154
promoted on social media, 53
and screen media use, 9–11
and sleep deprivation, 6, 37
and social media use, 70, 100
and TikTok use, 61
Design It For Us, 24
device(s)
blue light from, 40–41
boundary setting with, 26–28 (*see also* rules)
delaying giving devices of their own, 74–77
kids' opinions on limiting use of, 24
parental controls on, 161–63
psychological stimulation, 40
and sleep deprivation, 46
use of term, 14
see also technology(-ies)
Devious Licks challenge, 62
dinners, as no-phone zones, 116
Discord, 25, 64
disturbing social media content, 54, 65
dolphin parenting, 20–22
see also You're in Charge (Rule 1)
Doucleff, Michaeleen, 129–30
drama, on social media, 55, 168
driving, 50, 126–27, 141
see also Give the First Smartphone with the Driver's License (Rule 5)
drug content, on TikTok, 62
drug sales, through Snapchat, 63
Duolingo, 84

eating disorders, 11, 52, 53, 60
e-bikes, 140–41
Elachi, Aalia, 1
Elachi, Claudia, 86
Elachi, Dany, 1, 86
emotional safety, 174
empathy, 22–23
enforcing social media restriction, 66–68
Espejo, Devon, 171
"everyone else has one," 92–93
explanations of rules, 28–29

Facebook, 5, 16
face-to-face conversations, as no-phone zone, 116–17
family dinners, as no-phone zone, 116
fear of independence, 130, 147
fear of missing out (FOMO), 2, 60, 68
Find My Friends, 107
First Phones Should Be Basic Phones (Rule 4), 73–87
apps to allow, 83–85

First Phones Should Be Basic Phones (*cont.*)
- basic phones, 80–83
- choosing first phone, 79–83
- common obstacles and pushbacks, 85–87
- delaying giving devices of their own, 74–77
- flip phones, 77–79
- smartwatches, 80
- types of phones, 77–79

fish parenting, 20–22
flexibility with rules, 28–29
flip phones, 77–79
flying alone, 135, 141–42
followers, competition for, 54, 59
FOMO, *see* fear of missing out
freedom, *see* independence
Free-Range Kids (Skenazy), 134
friends, time with
- as excuse for late-night phone use, 47
- non-social-media options for, 67
- right before bed, 121
- and sleep deprivation, 46
- on social media, 69

Gabb Phone 4, 81
Gabb Phone 4 Pro, 82
Galloway, Scott, 16
gambling ads, 64–65
gambling sites, blocking access to, 102
gaming, 151–55
- addictive nature of, 16
- apps to allow, 84
- daily time limits for, 100, 101
- delaying use of, 75
- kids' reactions to controlling, 110
- sharing identity information when, 30
- and sleep deprivation, 46

gaming consoles, 39, 74, 151–55
Gates, Bill, 56
generational differences, 5
"gentle parenting," 20, 21
Gilzow, Noelle, 169–71
girls, sexualization of, 55
Give the First Smartphone with the Driver's License (Rule 5), 89–96
- "but everyone else has one," 92–93
- choosing and setting up smartphone, 93–95
- common obstacles and pushbacks, 95–96
- reasons for, 90–92

Give Your Kids Real-World Freedom (Rule 8), 125–47
- common obstacles and pushbacks, 143–47
- helping kids 3 to 12 develop independence, 129–38
- helping teens 13 to 18 develop independence, 138–43

goals
- of no phones during school days, 168–71
- of parenting, 23–25

going places alone
- for teens, 139–42
- younger kids' opportunities for, 132–38

Gray, Peter, 129, 134
Greenfield, Lauren, 49

Haidt, Jonathan, 128, 134, 152
happiness
- changing trends in, 5
- and device use, 74–75
- as parenting goal, 23
- and sleep, 6

harmful content, on social media, 52–54, 60

Heads Up Alliance, 86
Healthy Sleep Habits, Happy Child, 47
Hispanic teens, social media use by, 70
homework
as excuse to avoid chores, 146
as excuse to use devices, 164
low-tech, 179
and sleep deprivation, 46
using laptops for, 66–67
household chores, 137, 146
How to Live Dangerously (Cairns), 144–45
Hunt, Gather, Parent (Doucleff), 129–30

identity information, 30
independence
as goal of parenting, 23–24
helping kids develop (*see* Give Your Kids Real-World Freedom [Rule 8])
insomnia, 114
Instagram, 5, 11, 19
adults' understanding of, 25
and body image issues, 57
disturbing videos on, 54
harmful content on, 52–54
on "no" list for apps, 59–61
social comparison on, 56, 57
iPhone parental controls, 104, 106

Jobs, Steve, 56

Kennedy, Becky, 22–23, 32–33
keyed lockboxes, 43
kidnapping, 143–45
kids
flexibility and explanation of rules with, 28–29
helping develop independence in, 129–38
intentional addiction of, 16–17
response to structure and limits, 27
sleep needed by, 36–37 (*see also* bedtimes)
social media companies' income from, 68
use of term, 14
well-adjusted, 22
kSafe lockbox, 43

Lanahan, Owen, 35
Lane, Logan, 73
laptops
blocking social media sites on, 66–67
limiting YouTube on, 65
pairing phones with, 96
parental controls for, 106, 161–64
personal, 157–58
school, 2, 26, 155–57
used before bedtime, 115
laws
about childhood independence, 134–35, 145–46
technology regulation (*see* regulation of technologies)
legal adulthood, 50
Let Grow, 131, 134, 138, 146–47
LGBTQ+ teens, social media use by, 70
life satisfaction, 5, 57–59
Light Phones, 82–83, 94
likes, competition for, 54, 59
limbic (emotional) system, 50
location tracking, 108–9
lockboxes, 43
LOG OFF, 24
loneliness, 8
low-tech schools, 178–79

Martin, Luke, 1–2
Martinez, Shannon Foley, 127
Martinko, Katherine, 76, 77

melatonin, 41, 115
Mendes, Alexa, 56
mental health
 and age of smartphone ownership, 92, 93
 behaviors linked to, 8, 9
 changing trends in, 5
 and screen media use, 9–12
 and social media use, 57–59
 of teens, 8
 and TikTok use, 61–62
 see also specific aspects, e.g.: depression
Meta, 57, 60–61, 68
"minimal phone," 78
money, handling, 143
monitoring device activities, 102–3
 difficulty of, 26
 see also parental controls
Murthy, Vivek, 12

Nasca, Chase, 54
Net Nanny, 105, 163
No Electronic Devices in the Bedroom Overnight (Rule 2), 35–47
 common obstacles and pushbacks, 45–47
 consequences for ignoring, 46
 importance of bedtimes, 37–39
 sleep-disturbing monsters, 39–42
 sleep needed by kids and teens, 36–37
 steps for implementing, 42–45
no-phone zones, *see* Create No-Phone Zones (Rule 7)
No Social Media Until Age 16—or Later (Rule 3), 49–72
 apps to not allow, 59–65
 apps to possibly allow, 65–66
 common obstacles and pushbacks, 68–72
 damaging experiences with social media, 51–59
 features of problematic platforms, 59
 how to enforce, 66–68
notifications, turning off, 94–95
nude pictures, 11, 30

obstacles and pushbacks
 to Advocate for No Phones During the School Day, 179–82
 to Beware the Laptop—and the Gaming Console, and the Tablet, and . . . , 165–66
 to Create No-Phone Zones, 121–23
 to First Phones Should Be Basic Phones, 85–87
 to Give the First Smartphone with the Driver's License, 95–96
 to Give Your Kids Real-World Freedom, 143–47
 to No Electronic Devices in the Bedroom Overnight, 45–47
 to No Social Media Until Age 16—or Later, 68–72
 to Use Parental Controls, 109–11
 to You're in Charge, 32–33
online forums, blocking access to, 102
operating system controls, 103–5
OurPact, 105
outside time, 117–19, 138, 143

parental controls
 of Apple, 158–61
 apps to allow, 83–85
 apps to not allow, 59–65
 apps to possibly allow, 65–66
 on basic phones, 80–81
 choosing parent who sets up, 106–7
 in enforcing rules, 27
 for gaming consoles, 152–53

getting around, 99, 109–10
for laptops, 158–64
quality of, 71
to restrict hours of phone use, 43–44
setting up, 103–6
see also Use Parental Controls (Rule 6)
parenting, 4
with independent kids, 129
learning as you go in, 184
primary job in, 16
role modeling in, 32
styles of, 20–23
as unequal partnership, 23
see also You're in Charge (Rule 1)
Park, Diana, 35
Parker, Sean, 16
peer pressure, 13
permissive parenting (sea sponge parenting), 20–22
personal information, 30
personal laptops, 157–58
pet care, 135
phone calls, making, 137–38
phones
basic, 14 (*see also* basic phones)
delaying use of, 74, 76
flip, 79
for kids' safety, 85–86
smartphones, 14 (*see also* smartphones)
smartwatches, 80
taking away, 26–27
types of, 77–79
unsafe use of, 76–77
see also Advocate for No Phones During the School Day (Rule 10)
phubbing, 116–17
pictures/photos
of homework, 95
nude, 11, 30
of postings, 30
and sextortion, 52
on Snapchat, 62–63
social comparison with, 56–57
on social media, 71–72
Pinwheel phone, 82, 83, 98–99
Pornhub, 102
pornography
age of exposure to, 97
blocking access to, 102
on Discord, 64
kids' access to, 25
on TikTok, 62
viewed on school devices, 156
prefrontal cortex (self-control), 50
problem-solving ability, 128–29
promises kids make, 165–66
psychological stimulation, 40
pushback, *see* obstacles and pushbacks
push notifications, 59

Qustodio, 105, 160–61, 163–64

reading, benefits of, 119–20
Reasonable Childhood Independence laws, 134–35, 145–46
regulation of technologies, 2–3
lack of, 26
social media, 2–3, 12, 17, 24, 26, 49–50, 53–54, 59
young adults' lobbying for, 24
research on technology use, 4–11
see also individual topics
risks, assessing, 145
Roberts, Englyn, 61
Rodriquez, Selena, 11
role modeling, 32, 67
Romalewski, Kate, 1
rules, 3–4
Advocate for No Phones During the School Day, 167–82

rules (*cont.*)
Beware the Laptop—and the Gaming Console, and the Tablet, and . . . , 149–66
Create No-Phone Zones, 113–23
explaining, 28–29
First Phones Should Be Basic Phones, 73–87
flexibility with, 28
Give the First Smartphone with the Driver's License, 89–96
Give Your Kids Real-World Freedom, 125–47
importance of, 4–5
just talking vs., 14–17, 29
need for, 15
No Electronic Devices in the Bedroom Overnight, 35–47
No Social Media Until Age 16—or Later, 49–72
in parenting styles, 20–23
partial following of, 14, 183
reasons for having, 12–14
unclear consequences for breaking, 26–27
Use Parental Controls, 97–11
You're in Charge, 19–33
Russell, Molly, 53
Ruston, Delaney, 176
Rutherford, Mitchell, 167

school iPads, 156
school laptops, 2, 26, 155–57
schools
apps available when in, 101
low-tech, 178–79
parents' ability to effect policy change, 175–78
smartwatch use in, 80
see also Advocate for No Phones During the School Day (Rule 10)
school shootings, 181
Screenagers, 176
screen media
avoiding screen monsters, 39–42
conversations about dangers of, 29–32
defined, 9
and mental health, 9–12
see also specific media
screen time
and boredom, 121–23
kids' self-awareness of, 25
overall amount of, 164–65
when traveling, 151
scrolling, on problematic platforms, 59
sea sponge parenting, 20–22
self-harm, 52–54, 61, 62
sex, information about, 31
sextortion, 52
sexual abuse images, 64
sexual content
apps with, 99
on TikTok, 62
on X/Twitter, 64–65
sexualization, of girls and women, 55
Shaw, Russell, 170, 174
Shilts, Randy, 120
shopping, by kids alone, 132–33
Shulman, Liz, 180
Skenazy, Lenore, 108, 133–34, 144, 145
Skullbreaker challenge, 62
sleep
changing trends in, 6–8
and late-night phone use, 35, 39–40
limiting phone use before, 114–15
needed by age groups, 36–37 (*see also* bedtimes)
see also No Electronic Devices in the Bedroom Overnight (Rule 2)
sleep-disturbing monsters, 39–42

sleepovers, 136–37
smartphones, 2
  adults' understanding of, 25
  age for allowing, 66, 73–74
  average first ages of having, 19
  being "the only kid without," 86
  childhood changed by, 1–2
  choosing and setting up, 93–95
  defined, 14, 77
  kids' opinions on limiting use of, 24
  late-night use of, 35
  limiting YouTube on, 65
  and teen mental health, 5–6
  ways around parental controls on, 44
  young adults' opinions on, 24
  see also Give the First Smartphone with the Driver's License (Rule 5)
smartwatches, 74, 78, 80
Snapchat, 11, 12
  and body image issues, 57
  lack of privacy with, 30–31
  on "no" list for apps, 62–64
  sextortion on, 52
  18- to 27-year-old's opinions of, 23–24
  tweens' use of, 49
Snapscores, 63
Snapstreaks, 56, 63
social comparisons, 56–57, 61–62
social media
  addictive nature of, 16, 49, 60, 97
  age limit for use of, 49–50, 71
  algorithms of (*see* algorithms)
  average first ages of using, 19
  blocking, 102 (*see also* parental controls)
  childhood changed by, 1–2
  conversations about dangers of, 29–32
  daily time limits for, 99–100
  damaging experiences with, 51–59
  enforcing restriction of, 66–68
  kids' opinions about, 24
  kids' reactions to controlling, 110
  lack of regulation in, 2–3, 12, 17, 26, 49–50, 53–54, 59
  on personal laptops, 157–58
  privacy of, 30–31
  and sleep deprivation, 46
  and teen mental health, 5–6, 10–11
  young adults on regulation of, 24
  see also No Social Media Until Age 16—or Later (Rule 3)
social media companies, 2
social skills, 128–29
  decline in, 12–13
  in-person socializing, 6, 7
  and phone use during school, 174–75, 181–82
  see also friends, time with
Social Studies (documentary), 55
Spence, Alexis, 11, 66
sports
  and sleep deprivation, 45–46
  team posts on social media, 69–70
Spotify, 85, 96
streaks, 56, 59, 63
"Sturdy Leadership," 22
Subway Surfers, 84
suicidal thoughts, 11, 37, 61
suicide, 8
  and Discord use, 25
  and Instagram use, 61
  promoted on social media, 52, 53
  and social media use, 11
  and TikTok use, 61
summer downtime, 119–20

tablets, 66, 150–51
  delaying use of, 74, 75
  school, 156
  used before bedtime, 115

talking with kids
conversations about social media dangers, 29–32, 67–68
making rules vs., 14–17, 29
tech companies and executives, 56, 68
technology(-ies)
childhood changed by, 1–2
conversations with kids about, 29–32
and decline in social skills, 12–13
lack of regulation for, 2–3
protecting kids from, 13–14
research on effects of, 4–11
rules for managing, 3–4 (*see also individual rules*)
see also device(s)
teens
bedtimes for, 37–39
effects of technologies on, 4–11
helping develop independence in, 138–43
referred to as "kids," 14 (*see also* kids)
sleep needed by, 36–37
texts
lack of privacy with, 30–31
monitoring, 102–3
notifications for, 94–95
on WhatsApp, 65
third-party parental control software, 105–7, 162–64
"Tiger Mom" concept, 21
tiger shark parenting, 20–22
TikTok, 13, 17
18- to 27-year-old's opinions of, 23–24
disturbing content on, 54
harmful content on, 53
and mental health issues, 59
on "no" list for apps, 61–62
poor parental controls on, 71
tweens' use of, 49
time, as precious resource, 31–32
time limits
for gaming, 153
parental controls for, 99–101
time sink, with social media, 55–56, 70
toxic content, on X/Twitter, 65
tracking kids' locations, 108–9
travel alone, 135, 141–42
Trivedi, Anushka, 24
Troomi phone, 80, 82, 88
TVs, 39, 115, 150
tweens
illegal social media use by, 49, 51
referred to as "kids," 14 (*see also* kids)
self-harm among, 8, 9
Tyson, Amy, 179

uninvolved parenting (fish parenting), 20–22
unknown adults
and crime rates, 143–45
on Discord, 64
social media contacts from, 51–52, 59
when kids go places alone, 134–35
#Unsubscribed (Mendes), 57
Use Parental Controls (Rule 6), 97–111
choosing parent who sets up controls, 106–7
common obstacles and pushbacks, 109–11
monitoring kids' texts/online viewing, 102–3
setting up parental controls, 103–6
tracking kids' locations, 108–9
types of, 98–102

vacations, as no-phone zone, 117
validating kids' feelings, 22–23

videos
  Instagram Reels, 60
  on problematic platforms, 59
  and sleep deprivation, 46
  on social media, 71–72
  on X/Twitter, 65
  YouTube, 65–66
violent content
  blocking access to, 102
  X/Twitter videos, 65

Wait Mate, 86
Wait Until 8th, 86, 93
Waldorf schools, 56, 179
Wall Street Journal, The, 62
WatchTube, 80
websites
  blocking, 102
  laws for, 26
weekends
  bedtimes on, 37–38
  as no-phone zone, 119–20
WhatsApp, 65
women, sexualization of, 55
work
  paid, 126–27, 142–43
  volunteer, 142–43

X/Twitter, on "no" list for apps, 64–65

Yondr phone pouches, 169
You're in Charge (Rule 1), 19–33
  common obstacles and pushbacks, 32–33
  conversations to have with kids, 29–32
  difficulty of setting boundaries, 26–28
  flexibility and explanations, 28–29
  long-term goals, 23–25
  parenting styles, 20–23
  role modeling, 32
YouTube
  on "maybe" app list, 65–66
  on school laptops, 155, 156
  Spotify backdoor to, 85

ABOUT THE AUTHOR

Jean M. Twenge, PhD, a professor of psychology at San Diego State University, is the author of more than 190 scientific publications and several books based on her research, including *10 Rules for Raising Kids in a High-Tech World*, *Generations*, *iGen*, and *Generation Me*. Her research has been covered in *Time*, *The Atlantic*, *Newsweek*, *The New York Times*, *USA Today*, and *The Washington Post*. She has also been featured on *Today*, *Good Morning America*, *Fox & Friends*, *CBS This Morning*, *Real Time with Bill Maher*, and NPR. She lives in San Diego with her husband and three daughters.